THE LION WILL BECOME MAN

Alchemy and the Dark Spirit in Nature—A Personal Encounter

Keiron Le Grice

Zurich Lecture Series in Analytical Psychology

ISAPZURICH

Volume 9

CHIRON PUBLICATIONS · ASHEVILLE, NORTH CAROLINA

www.ChironPublications.com

Interior and cover design by Danijela Mijailovic
Printed primarily in the United States of America.

ISBN 978-1-68503-153-4 paperback
ISBN 978-1-68503-154-1 hardcover
ISBN 978-1-68503-155-8 electronic

Library of Congress Cataloging-in-Publication Data

Names: Le Grice, Keiron, author.
Title: The lion will become man : alchemy and the dark spirit in nature-a personal encounter / Keiron Le Grice.
Description: Asheville : Chiron Publications, 2023. | Series: Zurich Lecture series in analytical psychology; Volume 9 | Includes bibliographical references. | Summary: "In this compelling psychological memoir, Keiron Le Grice details his experience of a profound transformative crisis between 2001 and 2004. He explains how, by a sustained investigation of the root causes of his condition, he was eventually able to overcome the crisis, guided by instructive dreams and startling coincidences, illuminated by a series of symbolic paintings, and aided by his serendipitous discovery of the Gnostic text The Gospel of Thomas. Exploring the nature of the unconscious mind and the mysterious spiritual power behind his experience, Le Grice turns to the mystical symbolism of alchemy and the psychology of Carl Gustav Jung to set out a deep understanding of psychological rebirth and its relationship to the ongoing evolution of the Western psyche. The Lion Will Become Man gives a striking example of alchemy at work and reveals its great value as a guide to the complex developmental process that Jung called individuation"— Provided by publisher.
Identifiers: LCCN 2023042137 (print) | LCCN 2023042138 (ebook) | ISBN 9781685031534 (paperback) | ISBN 9781685031541 (hardcover) | ISBN 9781685031558 (ebook)
Subjects: LCSH: Individuation (Psychology) | Jungian psychology. | Alchemy. | Gospel of Thomas (Coptic Gospel)
Classification: LCC BF175.5.I53 L53 2023 (print) | LCC BF175.5.I53 (ebook) | DDC 150.19/54—dc23/eng/20231108
LC record available at https://lccn.loc.gov/2023042137
LC ebook record available at https://lccn.loc.gov/2023042138

For Kathryn

CONTENTS

Table of Figures

Table of Paintings

PREFACE

I wish to give my thanks to Murray Stein for the invitation to be the speaker for the 2023 ISAP Zurich Lecture Series, and to Steve Buser, at Chiron Publications, for the opportunity to publish this associated book. Together, the lectures and book reflect the range of interests that have preoccupied me, personally and professionally, for many years. These interests are centered on two overlapping areas: the process of psychological transformation that C. G. Jung called individuation and symbolic frameworks of understanding—notably, astrology and alchemy—that might enable us to make sense of our place in the universe and orient ourselves to the deeper powers shaping our life experience. While a number of my other books (including *The Archetypal Cosmos* and *The Way of the Archetypes*) are devoted to the theoretical formulation and application of a Jungian archetypal approach to astrology, *The Lion Will Become Man* is chiefly concerned with the psychological and spiritual significance of alchemy, which I apply to illuminate phases and themes of a transformative crisis in my own life.

As you will discover, this is a deeply personal book, recounting my struggle to come to terms with a protracted and complex death-rebirth process in the early 2000s. To convey anything meaningful about experiences of this kind one must bring in the personal dimension, for the path of individuation cannot be separated from what one is and the particular context of one's life. In what follows, I am able to write from inside the experience of transformation, as it were, to convey my first-person reactions and insights, and to give an indication of the life decisions and changes I was navigating at that time. But throughout, alongside the personal narrative, I show how the challenges and experiences I faced are related to collective factors and concerns, relevant to us all, and shaped by underlying archetypal and psychodynamic principles in our collective psychology. I aim to situate what I myself went through in the context of the larger process of the evolution of human consciousness and the spiritual challenge of our moment in history.

Alchemical treatises—comprising rather obscure descriptions of proto-chemical procedures interspersed with metaphysical speculations, mystical revelations, and mythic imaginings—are centuries old, from a vastly different time to our own bewilderingly fast-paced technological age. They can therefore appear arcane, outdated, and ostensibly of little relevance to the modern world. In sharing the example of alchemical themes emerging in my own life, I seek to counter this perception, and to demonstrate that alchemy, as a guide to rebirth processes, may be of immense value and interest to the individual today. Deviating from an orthodox Jungian approach, the book also provides an example of a process of individuation occurring outside of a psychotherapeutic setting, undertaken independently, without specialist support or guidance. Perhaps for some people this is the road that must be taken even if it brings more attendant challenges and dangers.

In addition to alchemy and individuation, the book covers an array of topics and themes intrinsic to Jungian psychology—archetypes, dream interpretation, synchronicity, mysticism, Christianity, Gnosticism, mythology, dialectical processes, the method of active imagination, death-rebirth experiences, possession states, symbolic expressions of the unconscious through art, facing the shadow, the integration of the Devil, the realization of the Self, and the nature of the divine. Yet it is written for a general audience, not as a specialist work for Jungians or other psychologists. My aim was to make the book accessible to anyone who might find themselves pulled into an existential crisis or a period of inner turmoil, seeking to better understand and navigate processes of psychological transformation in their own life.

I consider such a perspective especially important at a time when, at the hands of modern science and medicine, experiences of a mystical awakening, numinous "non-ordinary" states of consciousness, and existential crises are susceptible to unsympathetic misdiagnosis as symptoms of psychopathology and evidence of maladaptation to life. As Joseph Campbell once remarked, the mystic swims in the same waters in which the schizophrenic drowns—the territory is similar: symptoms of a progressive developmental transition might look from the outside very much like psychosis, regression, and disintegration. Correctly construing what one is experiencing is therefore imperative, as is the capacity to discern a larger trajectory of an inner psychological evolution running through the process. I hope to illustrate that alchemy can be of value in both respects. An informed reading of the symbolic language of alchemy, skillfully applied to our own experiences, might enable us to stay afloat, and to cross the turbulent waters of our unconscious psychic depths towards the yonder shore of transformed selfhood.

INTRODUCTION

In late 2001, I was pulled into a traumatic psychological crisis and process of transformation. The crisis led me into hellish suffering and darkness, through a kind of inner death, and forged within me a different self, fundamentally restructuring my personality, exposing me to the hidden depths of inner experience, and affording me insights into the nature of God and our collective psychological evolution. The main phase of the crisis lasted about three years, though the transformative process behind it still continues to unfold and impact me today. I write now, some twenty years later, having devoted my life to the study of the human psyche, both in my private explorations and inner struggles, and in my professional work as a professor of psychology and author of several books. From this vantage point, I will explain how I managed to free myself from the grip of this crisis and how I came to understand its meaning with the help of the obscure religious practice of alchemy and certain Gnostic insights, interpreted in terms of the psychology of Carl Gustav Jung. In sharing something of my own experience, I hope to illustrate the value of these perspectives in providing guidance and symbolic instruction that can help us come to terms with the spiritual powers and transformative processes shaping our lives.

* * * * *

Leading up to the onset of my crisis in late 2001, I had spent much of the previous several years denying my natural impulses and wishes, and generally living in a manner that was injurious to me, principally for

1

economic reasons—although I was well-intended: I hoped to raise money to enable me to leave my established profession as a computer programmer and embark on graduate studies in depth or transpersonal psychology and thus to carve out a new career in this area.[1]

The seeds of this crisis had been sown long before this time, however, for it arose out of conflict between my worldly ego and my deeper spiritual self. A decade earlier, between 1991 and 1994, during undergraduate studies in philosophy and psychology at the University of Leeds in England, I had passed through a revelatory, if somewhat destabilizing, awakening to the religious mystery and power shaping my life. My emerging spirituality was also inspired by my readings of the work of Carl Jung, Joseph Campbell, Alan Watts, Paramahansa Yogananda, the psychic Edgar Cayce, and others. At the same time, I became engrossed in astrology, undertaking a detailed analysis of my astrological chart as a way to better understand my personality, make sense of past experiences, and gain insight into what my future life path and vocation might hold. I was also experimenting with practices such as meditation and dream inter-pretation, and I wanted nothing other than to go further along this path and to advance my spiritual development. Alongside the usual college-student inclination towards hedonistic indulgence and freedom, my experiences and aspirations were often pulled inward, away from the world. This direction culminated in a sequence of powerful spiritual experiences when I was twenty-one, in my final year at university. Of these, one experience stands out above all others.

One night, in a dark and noisy, smoke-filled university disco, for some reason I fell into a state of deep discouragement. In that instant, sitting alone amidst a crowd of people, I spontaneously turned away from myself and my life, and I was overcome by the influx of what I can only describe as divine love. Suddenly, I knew, beyond all doubt, that I was in the presence of God and that my ultimate origin and destination were not of this world. I knew that I had come from elsewhere and that I belonged elsewhere. I was moved to tears, with a feeling of utter joy and liberation. I felt a divine homecoming and a longing to return to God, who, although I have never been religious in a traditional sense, I understood in loosely

Christian terms as my Father. Although it lasted only for a minute or so, the incomparable power and majesty of this experience left an indelible imprint on me and shaped my understanding of life thereafter.

Other religious experiences at that time were connected to what I understood to be the awakening of *kundalini* energy, conceived in the Hindu yogic tradition as the stirring of "serpent power" coiled at the base of the spine, bringing with it powerful tingling sensations in the body and a tremendous feeling of charge and uplift. Often, even reading an inspiring sentence that resonated with my awakening intuition of spiritual truth was enough to rouse in me numinous emotion and a surge of power.

Amidst these experiences, Italian psychologist Roberto Assagioli's *Transpersonal Development* became something of a guidebook for me, describing the process and stages of mystical awakening, which seemed to accurately reflect what I was going through in my life at the time.[2] Otherwise, however, despite the books I'd read, I had little in the way of context, lacking perspective and sufficient life experience to be able to adequately assimilate and integrate what I had been through. I felt I should act on my spiritual experiences, and build my life around them, but I did not know how to do this, or even how to talk about them with other people. For this reason, I kept them to myself.

After graduating from university in the spring of 1994, with financial pressures mounting and without a job or a real direction, I found myself in a difficult psychological state, even fearing for my sanity, as my spiritual aspirations and inward focus prevented me moving forward in life. Having experienced the rapture of spiritual transcendence, it was hard for me to commit to the mundane reality of the world. I became wrapped up almost entirely in my inner thoughts and process in a loop of endless insights, reflections, associations, and self-analysis. In late 1994, as I turned 22, I had moved temporarily to Queen's Park in London with my girlfriend, Kathryn (who was later to become my wife). Reading spiritually oriented books had by this point become almost habitual and felt increasingly detached from reality, providing an escape into the meaningful existence I craved but now undermining rather than supporting my psychological wellbeing. With student debt and the need to find work growing more insistent, I reluctantly took the decision to put all my psychological, spiritual, and astrological books away in boxes, and commit to "real" life in the world. I had in mind, from my reading of Jung, that I needed to give attention to the development of my ego, my conscious identity, for I did not feel settled enough in myself or anchored enough in the world to continue my esoteric explorations. I knew endless reading and ruminating on my inner processes were not helping me. I had to face the practical reality of my life situation. Thereafter, throughout most of my twenties, my focus on spiritual matters moved to the background of my life, although it never entirely left me.

From there, I eventually found my way into a career as a computer programmer for a large multinational corporation based in Nottingham, a medium-sized provincial city in the Midlands in England, and the closest city to my hometown. My studies of logic, as a philosophy undergraduate, had an affinity with the skills needed for programming, but I fell into this career more by opportunity than design. The position served me well for a while, but I knew from the first that I was ill-suited to day-to-day life in an office, and invariably I had to struggle against myself to continue. Indeed, by 1997, almost immediately after beginning the job, I succumbed to the debilitating condition of chronic fatigue syndrome, or ME, with persistent flu-like symptoms, severe headaches, extreme weakness, physical sensitivity, and exhaustion, which imposed an incapacitating physical restriction on my day-to-day life.[3] The condition persisted for over two years, but I struggled against the symptoms as much as I could, refusing to let them stop me from doing what I needed to. The illness was a clear signal, however, that the life energies working through me, expressed through the body, were strongly opposed to the way I was living and craved another, radically different life. I wrestled with myself because of this, and searched avidly for alternatives, but I was unable to find a solution other than to keep going.

Twice I left my position in the company, to travel and explore other possible careers, only to return when my finances ran low; and as the years went by it took more and more of a strained effort to remain in that life. I had to force myself to go to the office each day and once there I suffered

4

through each passing moment as I restlessly waited for the day to end, distracted only by mundane tasks and meetings that seemed to me utterly pointless. I persuaded myself that I had little choice but to endure this situation until I was in a financial position to make a change that would enable me to return to my initial interest in psychology and spirituality.

Towards the end of 2001, however, I could maintain this course of action no longer. As I came to realize, if I were not willing or able to change of my own volition, change would be forced on me. In December of that year, having recently turned twenty-nine, my emotional state became extremely agitated, even frenzied, with no outlet for the energies moving within me. Inevitably, I became sick again, with a virus that left me feeling spaced-out, weak, and psychologically uneasy. For some reason, although I had experienced more debilitating and severe symptoms before, this particular illness stirred in me the realization that I had absolutely no control over my physical condition: I could not make myself get well; I could not be sure I would ever become well; and I could do little, if anything, to prevent my demise and perhaps my death. Such morbid preoccupations were out of all proportion to the illness itself, and yet I could not stop them or reason them away. The realization of the lack of control left me panicked, and the panic, which I also could not control, became traumatic and later spiraled into an overwhelming dread. Although I resisted the descent into these states, suppressing the traumatic feelings as far as possible and trying to will myself to health, even throwing myself in desperation into attempts at various drastic life changes, all my efforts in the months to follow met with failure and served only to make my condition worse.

As the crisis unfolded, I stumbled into one disturbing state of consciousness after another, one strange physical symptom after another—including numbness in my face and limbs, hyperventilation, burning sensations in my body, digestive problems, dramatic heart palpitations and a racing heartbeat, acute nervous sensitivity, migraine headaches, immense pressures in my thorax, and cramps and "explosions" in my head. My usual capacity to control my personality began to collapse as did, for the most part, the structure of my life. Barely able to function in the world, the focus of my energy and attention became almost entirely absorbed in my psychological process and my symptoms, especially the ceaseless struggle against panic and dread, exacerbated by a fear of insanity and death.

At first, it was just a matter of survival. I had little sense of what was happening to me. All I could do was to try to withstand the symptoms and the trauma in the hope that they would subside, either naturally, of their own accord, or by some adjustment in my lifestyle and life aims. As the months passed, however, the crisis deepened rather than relented. I found myself in a stark confrontation with the depths of my personality that had been previously hidden almost entirely from my view. Having been torn away from my ordinary consciousness and way of living, I became embroiled in an encounter with the repressed emotions, instinctual drives, fantasies, resistances, and complexes that populated the unconscious side of my psyche—to put this in terms of Jungian psychology. It was an experience that was at once overwhelming, terrifying, and revelatory.

During this time, although I had not painted at all since childhood, I tried to give visual form to the extraordinary and often harrowing psychological states that arose, producing a series of paintings that, I was to discover, conveyed something of the hidden meaning of my experience. These paintings, together with many significant dreams and some startling symbolic coincidences ("synchronicities," as Jung called them), helped me to recognize the deeper transformative purpose behind my condition and eventually to navigate a way through it.[4]

The concept of the unconscious is central to depth psychology. It describes a dimension of our experience of which we are ordinarily unaware but that exerts a dramatic influence on us. According to Jung, whose ideas have most shaped my conceptual understanding of psychology, the unconscious is the source of the primary instincts and behavioral patterns of human experience and the transcendent spiritual factors that underlie and manifest through the meanings and myths by which we live. Jung called these factors *archetypes*, universal formative patterns and powers situated in the *collective unconscious*, common to us all. Archetypes are both spiritual and instinctual, giving rise to "numinous" experiences of mystery and power, populating the imagination with universal mythic motifs, and animating all we do. They are innate forms that are personified and symbolized by the gods and goddesses of myth, and evident in universal themes such as heroism and sacrifice, the conflict of the forces of light and dark, rebirth and the quest for rejuvenation, the confrontation with evil, and the yearning for union with God. Such archetypal themes manifest through our dreams, fantasies, pathologies, religious experiences, and in synchronistic coincidences. If one is to heal oneself of psychological division and become more whole, according to Jung, one must come to terms with the archetypes and the unconscious. This was a path that lay ahead of me as my crisis developed.

For the next three years, having become reconciled to the fact that I had to squarely face the crisis and accept it as part of my fate, I struggled incessantly to find a way to understand and overcome the extreme psychological turbulence and panic-fear that besieged me day and night—a process I will describe in greater detail in the chapters to follow. It was not until early 2004 that I felt I was at all ready to return to my life and to try to move forward; indeed, previous efforts to do just this had resulted in further trauma. But as 2004 unfolded I became tentatively confident that I had found a way to control, or at least hold at bay, the forces within me. And, with this, I remembered my long-held aspiration to study depth or transpersonal psychology and to forge a life within this field.

For me, this aspiration went hand in hand with the longing to move from Britain to live in America, which had been inspired by a period traveling in my mid twenties. The recovery of this calling and life passion, at the right moment, helped me emerge from my crisis. It gave an external focus to the energies I was grappling with and helped to redirect some of these energies away from my inner struggle. By this time, too, circumstances had shifted enough to make possible life openings previously unavailable to me. In 2003, in response to the pressure of our situation and to my desperate state of mind, Kathryn and I had sold our house in Nottingham and relocated to South Wales, to be close to her family. Benefiting from increases in property prices at that time, we were able to raise funds from the sale, and financing graduate study thereafter became a possibility—one I had not previously anticipated.

Shortly after, with the sense that I had little or nothing to lose, and willing to take a gamble on my life, I applied to enroll in graduate studies at the California Institute of Integral Studies (CIIS) in San Francisco. It was here, during my first semester of the M.A. Philosophy, Cosmology, and Consciousness program, that I became exposed to Jung's studies of the medieval practice of alchemy, especially his magnum opus *Mysterium Coniunctionis*. Today, as a professor of depth psychology at Pacifica Graduate Institute in California, this subject remains one of my primary areas of interest and teaching.

As I explored Jung's interpretation of the psychological significance of the alchemical texts during my first semester at CIIS, I was astonished to discover many parallels with my own experiences. Indeed, alchemy proved thereafter to be an invaluable source of insight and guidance for me, helping to illuminate the meaning of the transformative process I had been through and to participate in it as it continued to unfold.

As I began to appreciate more fully, alchemy is essentially concerned with the symbolism and description of processes of transformation, whose aims are ultimately of a religious order. Alchemy is a spiritual undertaking (a "mystic philosophy," as Jung puts it), and it is therefore to be understood as something far more than the literal attempt to create gold from base metal.[5] For this very aspiration, as Jung argues, may itself be read metaphorically as a symbolic portrayal of the inner process that might lead us to a spiritualized and transformed condition, not unlike a path of mystical realization. "Alchemy, with its wealth of symbols," Jung remarks, "gives us an insight into an endeavour of the human mind which could be compared with a religious rite, an *opus divinum*."[6] Although it appears to be concerned with the physical transformation of matter in a laboratory, its real concern, in Jung's view, was the transformation of the human being. The sought-after gold was the inner gold of realized selfhood. The observed changes in the matter, brought about by various chemical operations, named in Latin (such as *separatio, coniunctio, calcinatio, solutio, sublimatio*, and *coagulatio*), were actually a reflection or projection of the inner workings of the human psyche. The alchemist's obsessive work in the laboratory was a kind of sustained intense meditation, mediated through the imagination, and revealing an underlying affinity between matter and psyche, both of which seem to partake in the same basic patterns and themes of transformation.

The results of these endeavors are recorded in a diverse assortment of alchemical treatises, mostly originating in late medieval and early modern Europe, and comprising complex procedures and peculiar symbolism—often juxtaposing images and descriptions of chemical laboratory operations with scenes akin to myths and fairytales, featuring kings and queens, elemental and animal symbolism, and dramatic images of self-consumption, copulation, dismemberment, death, and resurrection.[7]

On first impression, the alchemical treatises appear to be so different from each other and so fantastical in content that it is impossible to make any sense of them. It took Jung's singular genius to recognize that, beneath the surface differences, the treatises all pertain to a single process of transformation. One could say that they are like different interpretations and portrayals of the same story or play, taking place in anything from three to five discernible acts or phases, named after colors: *nigredo* (blackening), *albedo* (whitening), *citrinas* (yellowing), and *rubedo* (reddening). (In later alchemical texts, from the fifteenth century, *citrinas* was often omitted. Certain texts also include *viriditas*, greening, occurring after the *nigredo*.) In carefully studying the phases and operations, Jung was able to recognize the common elements within the various renditions of the alchemical "story" and then explain how they can be used to inform and illuminate the deeper dimensions of human psychology.

More specifically, in terms of his own "analytical psychology," Jung found within the imagery of the alchemical texts a symbolic portrayal of the individuation process, with which he had been concerned all of his professional life. Individuation is a path of psychological transformation by which one comes to realize one's unique individuality, while over-coming inner disunity in an affirmative acceptance of the depths of one's character and the wholeness of one's experience. Individuation brings the conscious ego, the "I" principle, with its more or less exclusively personal sense of identity and conscious willpower, into relationship with a deeper principle of order and power in the depths of the unconscious psyche, which Jung called, somewhat confusingly, *the Self*. The result of this encounter is transformation: the ego dies to its former life, lived mostly for personal and socially conditioned aims, and is reborn in service of the Self, the incarnate "God-image" within us. For the Self, in Jung's view, is at once our own innermost uniqueness and the universal person within us, a godlike and eternal part of us. Individuation might thus be seen as something like a spiritual quest, as a modern alternative to a religious path that both draws on and goes beyond the Christian perspective of the Western world. It is a process that leads to self-knowledge, the discovery of deeper life meaning, and to the living of life in relationship to the numinous organizing powers that Jung called archetypes.

Although it could be said that individuation is a natural process, unfolding of its own accord, and that each of us is therefore individuating to a certain extent, it becomes that much more demanding and exacting when consciousness becomes involved. In certain cases, the onset of individuation proper might then take the form of a perilous crisis and a direct encounter with the contents of the unconscious, of the kind I passed through. In this form, individuation gives rise to experiences that pull one far away from one's ordinary awareness, into a realm of immense turbulence and magnified power, into an encounter with intoxicating fantasies and energies that can easily consume or destroy, as much as uplift and transform.

It is something of this kind, Jung discovered, that the alchemists were absorbed in, although they understood it in mythic and religious, rather than psychological, terms. Unintentionally, I had stumbled into the same dark process of transformation in my own life, which I came to understand as a critical phase of transition in my own individuation process. Alchemy, as I hope to show in what follows, afforded me a way to comprehend the phases and processes of this transition.

Jung himself had been through a period of profound inner disorientation, crisis, and transformation in his own life. His own much-discussed "confrontation with the unconscious" between 1912 and 1918, following his professional and personal break from Sigmund Freud, had jettisoned him into near insanity. He was inundated with a flood of stirring fantasies that broke through him as a religious revelation, which he subsequently labored to comprehend and articulate.[8] These experiences provided him, he later remarked, in reference to alchemy, with the "*prima materia* for a lifetime's work."[9] This period of Jung's life was detailed in the dramatic dialogues and imagery of *The Red Book*, an illuminated manuscript published in 2009 (based on his original *The Black Books*, subsequently published in 2020). It was only upon the discovery of alchemy in 1930, and the realization of its psychological import, that Jung stopped work on *The Red Book*. For in alchemy he felt he had discovered an historical counterpart to his theory of individuation, with the alchemical treatises understood as empirical records, in symbolic form, of the struggles of individuation mediated through the laboratory work.

Like the various records of the alchemists in the treatises they left behind, expressive of the unique nature of their individual experiences, each person who enters the dark underworld of transformation must find his or her own way through the labyrinth. The way must always be one's own, with its resolution in the terms of one's own life. But the process is not utterly unique for it partakes in recognizable themes, phases, and experiences. It is these that Jung sought to identify and explain in his alchemical writings, and it is these themes that I was able to recognize in my crisis of transformation.

The chapters to follow contain a selection of the dreams, syn-chronicities, and paintings that defined and informed my transformative struggle. Many of these were recorded in journals from that period in my life, in which I kept detailed logs of my experiences, attempts at self-analysis, and reflections on my life aims—mostly in an attempt to understand my crisis and free myself from it. In the interests of coherence, in some instances I have grouped together symbolic material expressing similar motifs even where these occurred at slightly different times or in a different order. For the most part, unless indicated in the text, the dreams and synchronicities occurred between 2001 and 2004. The majority of the paintings were done in a three-month period in early 2003, illuminating and anticipating my progression through the crisis. At the time I had little or no conscious idea of what I was painting; the meaning of the images only became apparent to me in retrospect. For comparison, the paintings are presented alongside a number of artworks from alchemical treatises, many of which are included in Jung's *Psychology and Alchemy*.

The accompanying reflections grew principally out of my personal study of Jungian interpretations of alchemy, and then later from teaching doctoral courses on this subject to students in the Jungian and Archetypal Studies specialization at Pacifica Graduate Institute. From both my personal and professional engagement with alchemy I was able to see for myself its great value, interpreted psychologically, for illuminating rare experiences of deep psychospiritual transformation in our lives. I have come to believe that an understanding of alchemy, and its forerunner, Gnosticism, might be of critical value to others undergoing similar experiences, trying to make sense of and find meaning in symptoms and sufferings that might otherwise be deemed pathological.

CHAPTER I
Sublimatio and Devil Possession

For most of my life, I have lived quite instinctively, in touch with and supported by a positive flow of feeling and fantasy. I have suffered when I have had to go against my emotions for any length of time, although to meet the requirements of living in the world this is often what we must do, of course. Indeed, in my own case I felt that life had called upon me from an early age to develop and cultivate thinking over and against feeling. My intellect had enabled me to prosper academically at school without much effort, and I naturally cultivated this as a strength and later perhaps as a crux, for as an adult it was certainly easier for me to read, think, plan, and analyze than it was to deal with the uncomfortable emotions and unconscious motivations that I had not yet addressed, or even recognized or consciously experienced, within myself.

To put this in Jungian terms, from adolescence, if not before, I had progressively built up a persona and sense of identity based on my intellectual capacities and an image of the person I believed I was and aspired to be. This persona was partly authentic, informed in my late teens by my awakening spiritual interests and my inner sense of the person I knew myself to be, but also, as for all of us, somewhat fabricated and conditioned, shaped especially by the innumerable values and impressions I had assimilated from without. I had found a place in society, or at least in the margins of society, in identifying especially with the youth counter-culture of the early 1990s, shaped by the "indie" and "grunge" music of the time. By early adulthood, I was comfortable in my assumed posture towards life and in my self-image, with elements of the spiritual seeker and freedom-loving outsider. I was concerned both with my spiritual life and having a good time. Although pulling me in different directions, these two pursuits were not overtly incompatible at the time, but there was much in my personality that I had not faced and not admitted to myself—much, in fact, of which I was entirely unaware.

At university, when I was about nineteen or twenty, I had a dream in which I entered a building with a tall tower, situated on the beach by the sea, and I climbed up to a library on the top floor, as nuclear explosions erupted outside and waves crashed all around. The ivory tower of the intellect, that is to say, had become my refuge as the unconscious world of instinct and emotion exploded all around me. From the safe confines of my intellect, I was mostly unaware of this at the time, although I had a hypnotic draw to the inner world. After university, in another dream I had taken off the well-worn 1970s beige suede jacket of my student years and stood exposed in the middle of an office. The persona ("coat") that had served me well for many years would mask me no longer, which led me into uncomfortable territory. I could no longer hide behind my rebellious outsider persona and the identity of my student life.

Since my spiritual awakening at university, I had "seen through" the spurious attractions of normal life and recognized the emptiness of the aims and aspirations by which people mostly lived. I therefore felt different from others in this sense. I was fierce in my derision of the ordinary world and in my independence and individualism. I was only able to withstand normal life under duress, forcing myself under the pressure of material circumstance to engage in a world governed by values and ideas in which I did not believe. Yet I wanted life, a full life of rich experiences—and this obviously entails earning money, forging a career, and pursuing worldly goals. I therefore had to commit to society and its values, whatever I thought of them.

As I struggled to make my way in the world in my twenties, eventually embarking on a profession in computing, I was living more and more in accordance with a strategic plan for my life, irrespective of how I actually felt about following that plan day by day. I had convinced myself, rightly or wrongly, that there was simply no alternative: I had to continue in my corporate computing position until I had earned enough money to have the opportunity to pursue the life I really wanted. I had no choice but to ignore and rationalize the unhappiness and restless boredom that afflicted me. This meant putting off the gratification of my inner feelings and passions indefinitely, for some future time. I could live again and be me again years down the line when I had created the conditions for this to happen. I saw many people around me living by a similar aspiration, often hanging on for retirement or for a time when they could make enough money to do something else, and many seemed well adapted to this proposition and way of life. But my feelings of restless revolt and longing for authentic life were urgent and powerful and could not be coerced, I would soon discover, much as I tried to ignore them.

It had even got to the point that I brushed aside ominous warning signs. In June 2001, after an interview to rejoin the company again in a new programming position, I had the following dream:

> *I see myself in an office wearing a gray shirt, which I often wore for work as a computer programmer. Images of Martin Heidegger, Adolf Hitler, and Nazis flash through my mind. I hear an ominous voice say "I will take the man that wears this!" I understand that I will be possessed by the Devil and that it will be many years before I will become free. I then see an image of myself as an older man with gray hair.*

The dream stirred in me great alarm and proved to be uncannily prophetic. But the alarm passed, and financial realities remained. I needed money to pursue the life that I wanted. What choice did I have? I was, albeit with some misgivings and inner resistance, determined to proceed as planned come hell or high water. In retrospect, I came to see this as a kind of willful hubris that led me precisely to hell and to high water.

I did not and do not see Devil possession literally, as being taken over by the Lord of Darkness as a disincarnate entity or a metaphysical principle, although the existence of such a principle is entirely feasible. But, as I was to discover firsthand, the Devil is certainly real as a personification of a psychological phenomenon, symbolizing the sum of forces in the psyche that have been dissociated, split-off entirely from consciousness and acting now with demonic autonomy and zeal, and thus capable of "possessing" the personality. The dissociation arises from a mode of being, a way of living, that has become dangerously one-sided, prioritizing rational consciousness, and consistently ignoring and repressing the claims of other dimensions of psychological experience, including the instincts and emotions.

It is a Devil possession of this kind that is depicted in *Faust*, as told by Christopher Marlowe and by Goethe, with the good doctor surrounded by his books in his study, suffocated by his learning and knowledge, making a deal with the devil Mephistopheles for the earthly fulfillment of desire in exchange for the eternal possession of Faust's soul.[10] "Mephistopheles," according to Jung, "is the diabolical aspect of every psychic function that has broken loose from the hierarchy of the total psyche and now enjoys independence and absolute power."[11] The chronic one-sided posture of ego-consciousness, heeding only the voice of rational intention, might summon a compensatory reactive force, arising from the unconscious, which can constellate with such irresistible power that it cannot be psychologically contained and starts to act compulsively and autonomously.[12]

My own Devil possession was brought about by a similar set of circumstances—a tremendous inner tension between reason and a practical concern for financial realities, on the one side, and the fire of my creative passion, feelings, and life energy, on the other. In 1999, on a break from full-time employment, Kathryn and I had spent three months touring the U.S., mostly in California and the other Western states. The entire experience was exhilarating, liberating, and healing, enabling me to recover from chronic fatigue syndrome and return to something close to full health. The trip was a return to nature, if only for a couple of months, allowing us to throw off many of the unnatural oppressions of contemporary life, and to come back to ourselves. For me, it also did much to inspire a creative flow of ideas that eventually took form in my first book, *The Archetypal Cosmos*. I felt that I had discovered the ideas and interests that were to be my life's focus.

Upon returning to Britain after the trip, Kathryn and I hoped that we could build our lives in the U.S. and were willing to try to make this happen. We had a particular affinity for New York (having stopped there twice for visits, in March and June of 1999), and in my case also for San Francisco, where I hoped to do graduate studies. But we knew that without employment visas (which were unobtainable for us at the time) and significant sums of money this dream was out of reach. Naturally, the thwarting of this life direction, especially having tasted freedom during our travels, led to a condition of acute inner dissonance, perhaps especially for me, as I had put myself back in the dire boredom of an office environment, which felt to me as if it were a sentence to be served. Again, I did this with the best of intentions. I saw no alternative, for we needed to raise money to have any chance of pursuing our dream.

Had I been able to move into the life I wanted at that point, or to remain close to nature in the wilderness of the U.S., there is no doubt in my mind that I would not have fallen into the hellish crisis. But I came to realize that life or God or the unconscious wanted more of me than to just live naturally, to find quiet contentment and fulfillment for myself. Happiness of itself does not usually lead to insight and self-knowledge, and to the revelation of life meaning. Suffering is the essential ingredient.

As I first experienced psychological difficulties, at the onset of my crisis, I had two significant dreams, giving further detail on the process that had been set in motion:

> *I climb a steep cliff face followed by Kathryn. I am eager and proceed easily to the summit. However, at the top events take a sinister turn as I realize we have become stuck, unable to climb down, and have unknowingly summoned or activated the Devil. I realize that it is too late to change this.*

> *I climb onto a large rock in a park in my hometown, Mansfield (in Nottinghamshire, England). I become stuck, afraid, and unable to climb down. Later, I fall into an underground cavern. Things from my childhood are there.*[13]

According to Edward Edinger, whose study of alchemy, *Anatomy of the Psyche*, I read in late 2004, dream images of climbing and ascent refer to the alchemical process of *sublimatio*, which involves the "raising up" of the matter in the alchemical vessel. It was associated by the alchemists with the element air—one of the four elements (with fire, earth, and water) described in ancient, medieval, and occult literature. *Sublimatio* is the airy ascent, and it thus symbolically suggests flight, rising up into the sky, as in the ascent of birds, which were often used to symbolically depict the operation. Psychologically, it is reflected in the capacity of human consciousness to elevate itself above the instinctual sphere, to detach itself rationally from the feelings and the body such that one is able to reflect upon and therefore rise above one's situation.[14]

These dreams suggest that the process of *sublimatio* had gone too far, that I had become too identified with the rational ego, and that I was unable to descend, to reconnect to the realm of feeling and instinctual dynamism. At the time, in my late twenties, in addition to the struggle to continue in my working life, after returning from my travels in America I

Figure 1. Mephistopheles in the Sky

Figure 2. The Devil, Rider-Waite Tarot Card

had been formulating many of the complex and dense theories that were to become integral to *The Archetypal Cosmos*, synthesizing ideas from a number of fields in the articulation of a new worldview.[15] I felt the tremendous intellectual strain of this endeavor, which, alongside my forced return to the corporate world, had left me nervously exhausted. I got to the point at which I could not read anything, not even a single sentence. I felt I had a physical block in my head, between my eyes, as if the cerebral cortex, responsible for thinking, were cramping up. The modern person, given to too much analytical, directed thinking, as Jung observed, is susceptible to suffer a "cramp of consciousness."[16] I was experiencing this acutely in physical form.

Living according to rational intention, forcing myself through intellectual willpower against my emotions and natural inclinations, I later realized, had eventually caused a dissociation of my ego from the energies and feelings of the larger psyche, which had become split-off and were no longer consciously accessible to me. It was these split-off energies, I came to understand, that led to the Devil possession. I had climbed high, perhaps too high, in the development of my thinking ego, relying on my intellect in an attempt to deliver me to a good life and to help me rise above my circumstances and background. I had savored high moments of freedom and exhilaration travelling around the U.S., which made it difficult thereafter to return to the humdrum reality of normal life. I had experienced too the transcendent heights of spiritual illumination that had thrust upon me an awareness of dimensions of reality outside of common view. In writing *The Archetypal Cosmos*, and in my earnest, if stalled, attempts to follow my spiritual calling, I had eagerly ventured out onto my own path, outside of the social expectations and collective consciousness of the culture. But this path is dangerous, I realized in retrospect, for, in forsaking the security and certainty of a life within the normal bounds of what is known, accepted, and expected, one becomes isolated and condemned to an uncertain and solitary path. I had elevated myself in this sense too, but now, whether by fate or by error, I had been trapped in my ego, and I could not, of my own volition, reconnect with the world of my emotions (as the dreams make clear, I was stuck). I was now to plummet into the depths where I was forced to come to terms with my psyche.

A *sublimatio* can take place of itself by the very nature of self-reflective consciousness, with its tendency towards objectification of the world and the rational distancing of subject from object. Living according to the dictates of reason, we can rise above our instinctive ways and natural urges—this is an achievement of the evolution of consciousness. Perspective and understanding arise too, as a result. But the distancing, when overdone, can become problematic and induce a kind of existential vertigo that causes us to plummet to earth—and below.

The human capacity for reflection is the defining characteristic of our consciousness. The ability to consciously intervene in and reflect upon the processes of nature and our own existence distinguishes us from animals, as far as we can tell. However, an excessive emphasis on thinking, analysis, rational will, and reflection at the expense of actually living and giving expression to the instinctual dynamisms of the body gives rise to a dangerously unbalanced condition, which might be imagined in religious terms as a kind of "sin" because it removes us from our natural state of unity with the world and nature. [17] It removes us from the state of *participation mystique* in which human consciousness is only hazily distinguished from the environment and the natural world—a condition that seems to have prevailed in our primal ancestors, before the development of the individual ego-selfhood we moderns now experience. It is a condition that is present in children too, before the developmental emergence of the ego. Young children live spontaneously and naturally, but for the most part unconsciously. As the ego develops, this naturalness is lost. Spontaneity is gradually replaced by considered action based on reason. The free expression of feeling is checked. The unconscious wholeness of life becomes then but a distant memory of our experience in times past. The alchemist Gerhard Dorn used the term *unio naturalis*, a natural union, to describe a condition of *participation mystique*. This "original, half-animal state of unconsciousness," as Jung put it, describing the *unio naturalis*, was characterized by an "inextricable interweaving of the soul with the body, which together formed a dark unity."[18]

To live according to the machinations of the ego is to intervene in the natural processes of life and thus in a sense to violate nature, breaking the hold of unconscious nature over us. Mythically speaking, the violation leads us out of the timeless, paradisiacal Garden of Eden into the horrors of the world of time, of subject-object duality, and to a sharpened aware-ness of the opposites, such as pleasure and pain, good and evil, light and dark. In my own case, the excessive development of ego-consciousness could be seen as the "sin" that led to possession by the Devil and a fall into the underground realm of the unconscious.

I do not think of sin here in moral terms, as the transgression against a moral or religious code, but rather as an inevitable consequence of our existence as beings separate from God and from nature, possessing our own portion of will and capacity for reason and independent judgment. The psychodynamics of this situation are addressed in Christian scripture.

If we act according to our own will, we cannot help but place ourselves at odds with divine will and thus fall into the sin of separateness. Indeed, according to the teachings of Jesus in the New Testament, we might conclude that this sin is intended. We are destined to fall into alienation, and it pleases God if we do so, for it is only through our alienation from God that we can come to know God. It is only through our expulsion from the paradise of Eden that we can come to know Heaven. The sin is therefore a blessed sin—the *felix culpa* of Christian theology. Alienation is necessary for the revelation of the divine in the light of human self-reflective consciousness. The parables of "the lost sheep" (Luke 15:3-7) and "the prodigal son" (Luke 15:11-32) point to this idea. The shepherd loves the lost sheep more than the other ninety-nine. The father throws a banquet and prepares the fatted calf on the return of the prodigal son from his profligate wandering, not in honor of the one who stays at home and does not dare the adventure of life and does not therefore engage his desire nature. In terms of the metaphysical drama of the Christian myth, one might say that God needs to bring the Devil into play, for the two are to be reconciled in human experience—an insight at the heart of Jung's interpretation of Christianity and one that has impressed itself on me since the time of my crisis.

At a collective level, we can see *sublimatio* in concrete form in the achievements of human civilization, set above and often against nature, with the building of great cities, with their skyscrapers and monuments, or in flight and space exploration. Through these immense acts of *sublimatio* human beings have elevated themselves above their earthbound condition thereby achieving a higher vantage point and expanded consciousness. Nowhere was this more apparent than in the 1960s space missions when human beings were first able to see with their own eyes the Earth as a single luminous living body in space. The modern rational mind, and the science and philosophy that it gave birth to, has brilliantly illuminated the world and raised human beings up, fuelled by the aspiration to liberate us from the grip of nature. But, as many have come to realize, the rise of civilization, the "ascent of man," has brought with it many problematic consequences too, not least the human domination of nature, now often objectified as something "other," separate from us and ripe for our exploitation. The ecological crisis, with the seemingly inescapable threat of the devastation of biological life on the planet, is a telling symptom of human misalignment with nature, and this is a consequence, in many ways, of an unchecked and unbalanced *sublimatio*.

ENDNOTES

[1] As defined on the British Psychological Society website: "Transpersonal psychology investigates spiritual practices and experiences, researching their value and their relationship to the models and concepts of psychology." See https://www.bps.org.uk/member-microsites/transpersonal-psychology-section (accessed February 24, 2020).

[2] Roberto Assagioli was the founder of psychosynthesis and a pioneer of spiritually oriented depth psychology.

[3] ME is a common abbreviation for myalgic encephalomyelitis.

[4] Synchronicity is a complex phenomenon that Jung defines in multiple ways. It is "a coincidence in time of two or more causally unrelated events which have the same or a similar meaning" and, more precisely, "the simultaneous occurrence of a certain psychic state with one or more external events which appear as meaningful parallels to the momentary subjective state." Carl Gustav Jung, "Synchronicity: An Acausal Connecting Principle" (1952) in Carl Gustav Jung, *The Structure and Dynamics of the Psyche*, volume 8 of *The Collected Works of C. G. Jung*, translated by R. F. C. Hull (Princeton: Princeton University Press, 1960/1969), pars. 849–850, 441.

[5] Carl Gustav Jung, *The Psychology of the Transference* (1954/1966), translated by R. F. C. Hull (Princeton: Princeton University Press, 1974), par. 354, 5.

[6] Carl Gustav Jung, *Mysterium Coniunctionis: An Inquiry into the Separation and Synthesis of Psychic Opposites in Alchemy*, volume 14 of *The Collected Works of C. G. Jung*, second edition (Princeton: Princeton University Press, 1970) par. 790, 554.

[7] Among the most prominent alchemical practitioners were Maria Prophetissa (1st–3rd centuries CE), Zosimos the Greek (circa 300 CE),

George Ripley (1415–1490), Paracelsus (1493–1541), Gerhard Dorn (1530–1584), John Dee, (1527–1608), and Michael Maier (1568–1622).

[8] See, Carl Gustav Jung, *Memories, Dreams, Reflections*, recorded and edited by Aniela Jaffé, translated by Richard and Clara Winston (London: Flamingo, 1983), chapter V, "Confrontation with the Unconscious."

[9] Jung, *Memories, Dreams, Reflections*, 225.

[10] In an analysis of the dreams and visions of physicist Wolfgang Pauli, Jung connects the appearance of "an employee with a pointed beard" to the figure of Mephistopheles who was "employed" by Faust and who represents the intellect that is functioning autonomously and daemonically. See Carl Gustav Jung, *Psychology and Alchemy*, volume 12 of *The Collected Works of C. G. Jung*, second edition, translated by R. F. C. Hull (Princeton, Princeton University Press, 1968), par. 88, 69.

[11] Jung, *Psychology and Alchemy*, par. 88, 69.

[12] As Jung explains:

> The further the conscious situation moves away from a certain point of equilibrium, the more forceful and accordingly the more dangerous become the unconscious contents that are struggling to restore the balance. This leads ultimately to a dissociation: on the one hand, ego-consciousness makes convulsive efforts to shake off an invisible opponent . . . while on the other hand it increasingly falls victim to a tyrannical will . . . which displays all the characteristics of a daemonic subman and superman combined. Jung, *Psychology of the Transference*, par. 394, 31.

[13] Jung discusses the motif of a return to the world of childhood or "children's land" in his analysis of physicist Wolfgang Pauli's dreams and visual impressions (see especially dreams/impressions 10 and 11 in Jung, *Psychology and Alchemy*, pars. 73–77, 58–60). The same motif is explored by Joseph Campbell in *The Hero with a Thousand Faces* (London: Fontana Press, 1993), 17.

[14] Edward Edinger, *Anatomy of the Psyche: Alchemical Symbolism in Psychotherapy* (Chicago and La Salle, IL: Open Court, 1991), 118, 126–127. Both Jung and Edinger cite the example of Nietzsche as a paradigmatic case of excessive *sublimatio*.

[15] Keiron Le Grice, *The Archetypal Cosmos: Rediscovering the Gods in Myth, Science and Astrology* (Edinburgh, UK: Floris Books, 2010).

[16] Carl Gustav Jung, "Commentary on 'The Secret of the Golden Flower'" (1957) in *Alchemical Studies*, volume 13 of *The Collected Works of C. G. Jung*, translated by R. F. C. Hull (Princeton: Princeton University Press, 1967), par. 20, 17.

[17] As Jung remarks: "Egocentricity is a necessary attribute of consciousness and is also its specific sin." Jung, *Mysterium Coniunctionis*, par. 364, 272.

[18] Jung, *Mysterium Coniunctionis*, par. 696, 488.

CHAPTER II
The Descent of the Western Ego

Despite the particular circumstances and personal decisions that led to the onset of my crisis, it was also related to the collective situation facing many people today, at this moment in our history and evolution. It was a reflection, albeit in quite extreme form, of the modern existential predicament, with the prevalence of all manner of psychological ills, documented by writers and clinicians from the nineteenth century onwards: alienation, estrangement, meaninglessness, angst, ennui, nausea, and dread. The modern ego, Jung remarked, has become rootless, that is, disconnected from the instinctual roots of its own being and from its deep historical and ancestral roots in the past. The *sublimatio* has elevated us, and to an extent liberated us from our enmeshment in nature, but the modern ego has become dizzy and disturbed from the heights, trapped in a solipsistic world, detached from the larger reality of cosmic meaning.

In the mythic scenes of the alchemical treatises, ego-consciousness is symbolized by *Sol*, the sun, suggesting the "light" of consciousness and the capacity of self-reflective awareness to illuminate our experience. The symbolic connection is not peculiar to alchemy. A number of thinkers have depicted the rise of Western civilization and the rise of the modern ego-self using the analogy of the sun's journey through the sky. In a glorious ascent from the night-time darkness below the horizon, the sun reaches its pinnacle, just as the ego emerges, over the course of our collective psychological history, to an apex of differentiation. The modern individual, the solar ego, comes to know acutely the experience of separateness—of its identity, will, judgment, and awareness—as it stands alone, the luminous center of its own world.

The trajectory of egoic development—with the human being emphasizing its own will and estranged from the larger matrix of cosmic or religious meaning—culminated, perhaps inevitably, in nihilism, with the purported loss of all meaning. This development was dramatically captured in 1882 by Friedrich Nietzsche's proclamation of the "death of God," in *The Gay Science*, in words uttered by a "madman."

> "Whither is God?" he cried; "I will tell you. *We have killed him—* you and I. All of us are his murderers. But how did we do this? How could we drink up the sea? Who gave us the sponge to wipe away the entire horizon? What were we doing when we unchained this earth from its sun? Whither is it moving now? Whither are we moving? Away from all suns? Are we not plunging continually? Backward, sideward, forward, in all directions? Is there still any up or down? Are we not straying as through an infinite nothing? Do we not feel the breath of empty space? Has it not become colder? Is not night continually closing in on us? Do we not need to light lanterns in the morning? Do we hear nothing as yet of the noise of the gravediggers who are burying God? Do we smell nothing as yet of the divine decomposition? Gods, too, decompose. God is dead. God remains dead. And we have killed him."[1]

Thus the path of the ascent of the ego results, if carried to its extreme, in a terrifying sense of utter existential disorientation, with all reference points—cosmological, moral, metaphysical, religious—wiped away. Nietzsche experienced this profoundly, in the depths of his being; his philosophy was a confession of his own existential and psychological condition. In a virulent repudiation of past truths, especially of religion and morality, and with an aspiration to climb ever higher in an evolution towards the *Übermensch* (the Superman or Overman), Nietzsche saw himself as "six thousand feet beyond man and time,"[2] looking down in judgment on the banal littleness of the mass of humankind from the astral heights of philosophical realization—a dangerously one-sided condition, as Jung points out.[3] In another dramatic scene, in "Of the Vision and the

Riddle," in Part III of *Thus Spoke Zarathustra*, Nietzsche narrates an exchange between his alter-ego Zarathustra and the "Spirit of Gravity," an adversary taking the form of a repugnant crippled dwarf. In resisting the dwarf's warning that he would fall to earth like a stone, Zarathustra repudiates the principle that seeks to impede or prevent his upward trajectory into the greatness of the *Übermensch*, perhaps in the process, however, severing his connection to the earth and to the grounding provided by the humdrum, everydayness of ordinary reality.[4] As Jung has argued, Nietzsche could not accept his littleness and weakness, symbolized by the dwarf, which represent the compensatory shadow side of his ideal of greatness, self-overcoming, and strength—although other conclusions might be drawn here too.

But, with a keen sense of his own destiny and our collective future, Nietzsche also serves as the prophet of an impending descent in a critical moment of transition ("the great noontide") in the trajectory of the life course of the ego and of human civilization. Nietzsche has Zarathustra say to the sun: "I must descend into the depths: as you do at evening, when you go behind the sea and bring light to the underworld too, superabundant star! Like you, I must *go down*."[5] For as surely as night follows day, so the solar ego continues on its course, and thus begins its descent into the darkness of the underworld. The alchemical opus, I came to discover, describes this transformative underworld journey in extraordinary detail.

In early 2002, besieged by dread and panic, and beleaguered by a multitude of seemingly pathological symptoms, as I struggled to come to terms with the dark experiences I had fallen into, I imagined at first that I had committed some grave error for which I was now being punished, for it felt as if I were in a state of hellish damnation. I naturally came to regret my decision to continue in my corporate role. I recalled the Devil possession dream and berated myself for not having heeded the warning. How could I have been so blind, so foolish, so reckless? I had activated an irreversible process from which I could not free myself. That realization too stirred in me a claustrophobic panic that I could not bear. I felt as if I were imprisoned by an unseen jailor with no prospect of release and subject to suffering that felt at times like torture. I was trapped within myself, unable ever to feel free again, to be whole again—or so it seemed to me.

However, in other moments, later in the process, I also came to see my experience in a more positive light. Although I wished each day that my symptoms and suffering would leave me and that I could return to my former feeling of psychological freedom and relative happiness, I recognized that I was passing through an existential crisis that, while acutely personal, was an expression of an evolutionary progression of some sort. I had the sense that it was not just my personal ego that was the object of the transformative crisis, but the ego in general—that I was embroiled in a transformative experience that was birthing a new kind of self, perhaps a new kind of human being. I was a carrier for something beyond me, a participant in a critical phase of transition. Nietzsche's vision of the coming *Übermensch* and Jung's understanding of the Self were at the forefront of my mind in these moments.

It would have been easy to delude myself about this, of course. From an outside perspective, I was just sick and depressed, in need of rest and medication, unable to function at even a basic level. But in my inner evaluation of what was happening, available to me in fleeting moments of insight, the experience only made sense in terms of a developmental spiritual transition. As I deepened into the experience month by month, so this assessment became more compelling—although it was to be severely challenged by circumstances and my own failed attempts to flee from or reverse the process. In time, my self-judgment about what had happened dissipated, for I came to the opinion that I had effectively been set-up by life, by the unconscious, perhaps by God. I felt that it was meant to happen, that I had to experience it, and it was in a sense an inevitable consequence of who I am. The decisions I had taken and the path I had committed to were a reflection of my character. So even though it appeared to be the case that free will was in play, the "free" choices I had taken were already conditioned by my essential nature. Character, it has been wisely said, is destiny.[6]

* * * * *

30

What is most peculiar about alchemy is that it juxtaposes images and descriptions of chemical operations performed on matter in the laboratory with fairytale and mythic scenes. The imagination represents the transformations of the matter in various kinds of symbolic imagery, including celestial and anthropomorphic symbols of the protagonists in the alchemical drama. For instance, in one such symbolic expression, certain alchemical treatises feature a king. We can imagine that the king, as the ruler, depicts the established state and form of the matter before it is subjected to the various procedures that will break down this form. The matter is secure in its established state just as the king is initially secure in his position. As the form of the base material is broken down, however (or needs to be broken down), so in the mythic imagination of the alchemist the king becomes sick, his kingdom falls into ruin, and in time he dies. The old king has to die, just as the established form of the matter has to be destroyed if the gold of the philosopher's stone—the aim of the alchemical opus—is to be attained.

These happenings in the alchemical vessel and in the king's court have a psychological corollary too, for the king also symbolizes the dominant or ruling principle of ego-consciousness that is responsible, in part, for the dissociation from the instincts. "The king," Jung remarks, "personifies a hypertrophy of the ego which calls for compensation."[7] The king, we can imagine, elevated or even inflated by his position, recognizes no authority but his own, rules his kingdom with autocratic power, and thus sets himself up for a revolt. As the alchemical drama unfolds, he must come to recognize that he is there to serve his kingdom and bow before an authority above and beyond his own. Herein lies the way to the king's rejuvenation and renewal.

So it is too for the ego, the ruler of consciousness, who like the king is to be subjected to various sufferings and transformative procedures at the hands of the kingdom of the larger psyche and the ultimate authority of the Self—the central organizing principle and totality of what we are. In the language of archetypes and individuation, the psyche compensates for the hypertrophy of the ego with an irruption from the unconscious, which makes itself known to us first in the form of the shadow, the archetypal figure that personifies the dark half of the personality.

In Jung's view, the human personality is not a singular entity, as we tend to assume, but comprises a multiplicity of different characters and centers, which exist unconsciously within us. We usually do not know of these centers, or archetypes, unless we are compelled to recognize them and relate to them in the course of the individuation process.

The shadow is the first archetype to present itself during an encounter with the unconscious, which is usually instigated by the work of psychotherapy or occurs spontaneously through a crisis, as in my own case. The shadow constitutes the inferior personality, comprising all those aspects of our experience about which we feel guilt, shame, embarrassment, weakness, and so forth, and all those traits deemed taboo or morally unacceptable and thus screened out of conscious awareness. It is associated with the realm of the repressed unconscious, comprising affects and attitudes, compulsions and motivations, that we have been unable or unwilling to face, and that often go unrecognized. The shadow also has its roots in our collective psychology, personifying dimensions of experience considered primitive, barbaric, and evil, and thus incompatible with the norms and expectations of civilized life.

Jung discovered that a confrontation between the ego and the shadow, of the kind I was experiencing, often produces a "dead balance, a standstill that hampers moral decisions and makes convictions ineffective or even impossible." It creates a situation in which "everything becomes doubtful" and, in a "torn and divided state" the person loses the capacity for decision, or the impetus to act in the world.[8] The shadow (and the other archetypes that stand behind it) makes a claim on the life and personality that is equal to or perhaps greater than that of the rational ego. The ego might cling to its old ideals and strategies, but the shadow is a presence that cannot be ignored, for it represents the power of one's unlived life, ignored feelings, and repressed energies that can rise up with an avenging zeal, threatening to seize control of the personality. Under the influence of the shadow one might desire things and entertain courses of action that are contrary to one's better nature and sober, clear-minded judgment.

One's primitive side rears its head, comprising compulsive desires and fears that have not surfaced before or have not been faced or acknowledged—impulses that fall within the collective shadow of civilization as much as within the personal shadow.

In my own case, the demands of those impulses and urges, dismissed or unrecognized for so long, were now to be reckoned with. I oscillated between, on the one hand, assenting to the transformative process and remaining true to my highest spiritual ideals and possibilities, and, on the other hand, seeking flight from my suffering, in the pursuit of some alluring image or yearning that promised a quicker and easier route to fulfillment and an end to suffering. Around this time, I would dream of being pursued or threatened by figures who seemed to symbolize the shadow—werewolves, beasts, wild animals, dark figures, and (in a personal rendering of the instinctual power of shadow) often the Incredible Hulk of the 1970s television show, which had gripped and scared me as a child. The Hulk is an arch personification of anger and rage, unconsciously possessing the rational and reasonable conscious personality, for better and for worse.

To put this another way, although one side of my personality had been blessed with spiritual experiences and wished to live in accord with these, there remained much of my psyche that was anything but spiritual, existing in an unredeemed state. I would also sometimes dream of scenes from university in which feces were smeared across the walls of my room, needing to be cleaned, which I took to imply that I was still unconsciously dominated and motivated by residual attitudes from that time in my life that were obstacles to moving forward and were now at odds with the person I needed to become. My psyche was divided against itself, and this fractious disunity was to break out into an outright warring conflict during my crisis.

As incomprehensible as it might now seem, one option for me at the time, as I searched for a solution to my deepening crisis during the first half of 2002, was to stay indefinitely in my position as a computer programmer, maintaining a salary that could give me security and a comfortable existence, allowing me to meet my responsibilities and to pursue the ordinary aims and satisfactions of life, but thereby forsaking my passion or redirecting it into other channels. It would have been easy to believe, in my troubled and confused state of mind, that my spiritual aspirations and my passion for a career in depth or transpersonal psychology in the U.S. were the cause of all my problems. I had overreached and paid the price. I had set my sights too high, and I needed to be more modest in my ambitions. It would be better for me to live an ordinary life, to settle for what I had rather than sacrificing any more in some ill-advised pursuit of a life based on a mere wishful fantasy. Such reasoning presented itself for serious consideration, and was sometimes persuasive to me, for often I could not think clearly or access my true feelings. Jung has described this kind of reaction to the crisis of transformation as a "regressive restoration of the persona" in which, feeling defeated by life, one reverts to a simpler mode of existence, an earlier and more limited version of oneself, but in so doing condemns oneself to a painful neurosis.[9] For, in responding this way, an essential part of one's nature—the transpersonal power that has found no adequate place in one's life—will perforce protest against the artificially imposed restriction one is placing upon oneself.

One night I dreamed I was with a throng of people in a city street in Nottingham in a scene that I knew was connected to my job in the corporate world. The crowd swarmed all around and then charged in a stampede. I was swept up by it and trampled. The message to me was clear: If I were to remain in my corporate position, I would be forsaking who I really am, and I would be lost in the crowd, trampled by the herd, crushed by the mass. Individuation, as I knew well from my reading of Jung and Campbell, entails a path of individual differentiation away from the common crowd. It takes one off the beaten track into the dark forest, not into the marketplace. I also knew that getting lost in the dark forest was often part of the spiritual adventure. One must lose oneself and go astray in order to find oneself. Of course, it was one thing to comprehend these truths intuitively or intellectually but quite another to remain faithful to them amidst the confusion and suffering of my condition. But I felt compelled to overcome my crisis whatever it took.

I thus concluded, perhaps belatedly, that I should leave my position in the company. I tended my resignation in the summer of 2002, thereby severing the main connection I had with the world. Leaving my job was to plunge me more deeply into myself, and deeper into my crisis. As unpleasant and painful as this was, I came to appreciate that it was the only course of action that could bring about a resolution. One cannot go back; one must go down and through, out of the other side of the crisis.

The competing aspects of the psyche, manifesting initially as the conflict between the ego and the shadow, can create an irresolvable tension between differing clusters or "complexes" of values, feelings, desires, and aims. This state of irresolution gives rise to a damming up of the flow of libido, producing what Jung calls *regression*, as psychic energy is driven inwards, charging and activating the unconscious.[10] The alchemists, it occurs to me, must have experienced something like this inner conflict in their work for they undertook the opus with a devout religious attitude, giving themselves day after day to the intense labor of working in the laboratory in the obsessive quest for the philosopher's stone. We can imagine that other aspects of their personalities would have welled up in revolt against this singular dedication to the opus. The alchemists would surely have been subject to inner voices suggesting they abandon their work and live differently, and to fantasies and desires for the good things of life unavailable to them amidst their austere spiritual labors. Thus a stand-off would have been created, charging the unconscious to such an extent that the matter in the *vas alembic* and the alchemist's psyche acted almost in sympathy, the one reflecting the other.[11] Just as the alchemist was violating the natural state of the matter in the alchemical vessel (by cutting it apart, heating it, dissolving it, and so forth), so the alchemist's own psyche was violated by the performance of the work. In committing solemnly to the work to the exclusion of all else, the alchemists' natural inclinations would be contained, checked, and resisted, such that the grip of natural instinct and desire over them could eventually be broken. The natural mode of existence—the *unio naturalis*—would thus be forsaken in the quest for spiritual gold.

ENDNOTES

[1] Friedrich Nietzsche, *The Gay Science: With a Prelude in Rhymes and an Appendix of Songs*, translated by Walter Kaufmann (New York: Vintage Books, 1974), section 175, 182.

[2] Friedrich Nietzsche, "Ecce Homo: How One Becomes What One Is" in *Basic Writings of Nietzsche*, translated and edited by Walter Kaufmann (New York: The Modern Library, 2000), 751.

[3] For Jung's discussion of Nietzsche, see, for example, Carl Gustav Jung, "On the Psychology of the Unconscious," in *Two Essays on Analytical Psychology*, second edition, volume 7 of *The Collected Works of C. G. Jung* (Repr., London: Routledge, 1990), par. 36–43, 31–35.

[4] Friedrich Nietzsche, "Of the Vision and the Riddle" in *Thus Spoke Zarathustra*, translated with an introduction by R. J. Hollingdale (London: Penguin, 1969), 176–180.

[5] Nietzsche, "Zarathustra's Prologue" in *Thus Spoke Zarathustra*, 39 (emphasis in original).

[6] Quote attributed to Heraclitus.

[7] Jung, *Mysterium Coniunctionis*, par. 365, 272.

[8] Jung, *Mysterium Coniunctionis*, par. 708, 497–498.

[9] Jung, "The Relations between the Ego and the Unconscious" (1928) in *Two Essays on Analytical Psychology*, par. 254–259, 163–168.

[10] Jung discusses the regression of libido in detail in his essay "On Psychic Energy" (1948) in *On the Nature of the Psyche* (London and New York: Routledge, 2001), par. 60–76, 37–47.

[11] The *vas alembic* is the alchemical vessel.

CHAPTER III
Dread, the *Nigredo*, and the Opposites

During 2002 and 2003, in the midst of the crisis, I sometimes found myself unable to read, write, or even think due to the sensation of "blocks" in my head. Many days and nights were an ordeal due to the severity of my physical symptoms. My intellectual capacities were severely impaired and yet it was crucial, I knew at some level, to find a way to comprehend as best I could the meaning of what was happening. To this end, I had to rely on my imagination and my feelings, as crude and confused as they were. One response was the urge to try to give form to my feelings through painting—something that I had never before considered. The intention was vague: I knew only that I would make brush strokes on paper. As my wife is an artist, materials were readily available to me, and I was able to paint as and when I needed to. Sitting with brush in hand in front of a blank sheet of paper, I had no idea what I wanted to paint. I simply chose colors and allowed my hand to be guided by whatever thought, feeling, or image came to me. There was no strategy or design in this whatsoever. Painting was simply a survival mechanism, something I could try when all else had seemingly failed. Invariably, the act of giving form to my experience, however clumsily, gave me a feeling of minor satisfaction, as if I had gained an objective perspective on my experience and caught a glimpse of the meaning and developmental trajectory underlying the surface pathology. I approached the project with the naivety of an unskilled craftsman. Although, I have been exposed to a lot of paintings in galleries and museums on visits with my wife over the years, and developed an aesthetic sense that way, I have virtually no technical ability, for I had not done any painting since elementary school. In retrospect, I can see that my lack of skill and experience freed me from any concern with form or quality, which permitted a greater degree of spontaneity and authenticity.

The following painting was among the first I produced.

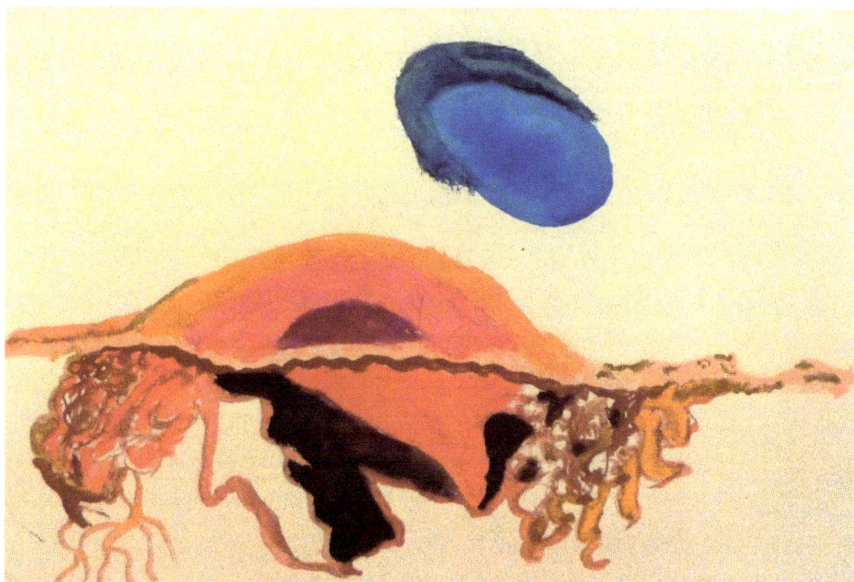

Painting 1. Underground and Blue Spirit

The motif of the descent is suggested here—the setting sun (the alchemical *Sol*) could be seen as a symbol of the descent of consciousness into the darkness of the underworld below the horizon. At the time, although I knew I had fallen into the pits, I was also aware of the upsurge of contents from the unconscious. I felt that something was breaking out of me, pushing toxins to the surface, like a boil on the skin, which is perhaps conveyed in the painting.[1] I was also suffering acutely with the dissociation of my consciousness from my feelings, suggested in the painting by the blue shape. This also suggests depression. Indeed, I had a dream around this time in which, as in the painting, a detached blue spirit—an entity like a cloud or energy field hovering in the air—entered into me. The dream and the painting gave form to what I knew but had not really articulated: I was in some way altered. The clarity of my consciousness was gone. I felt flat, devoid of any flow of feeling and life energy, as if part of me had vanished or was now affecting me adversely as a possessive and potentially destructive force. I was mere witness to this; there was nothing I could do to prevent it or reverse it.[2]

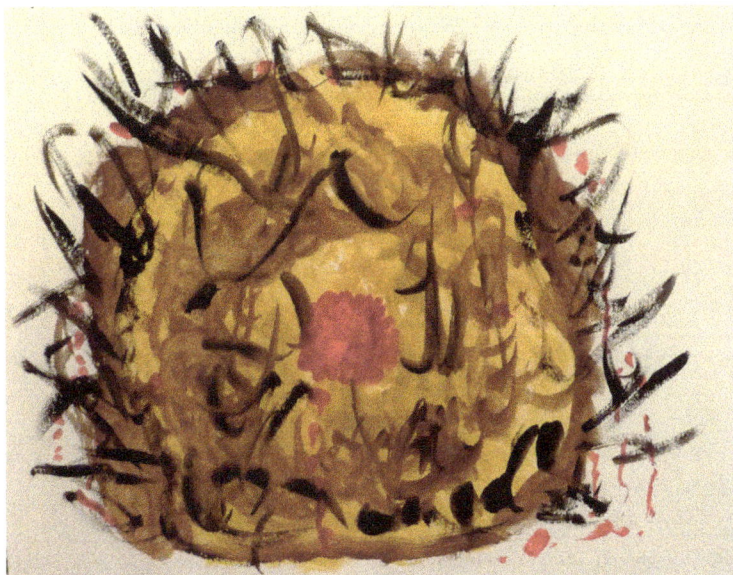

Painting 2. Conflagration and Blistering I

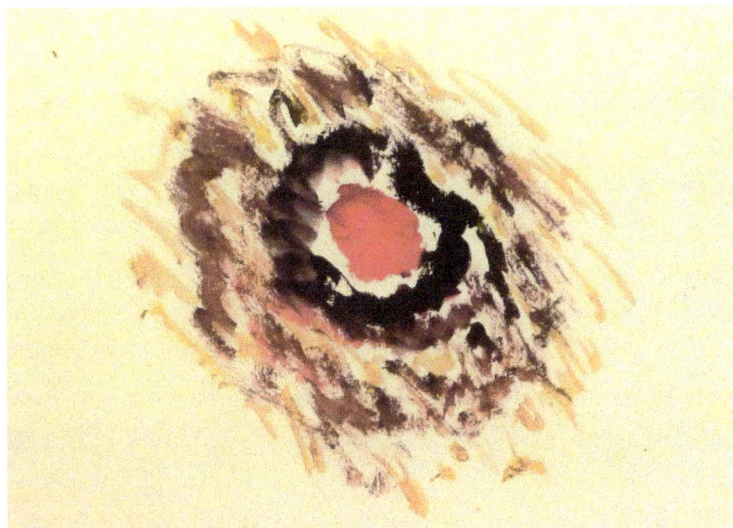

Painting 3. Conflagration and Blistering II

Energies and drives that once supported and motivated me, and that would have been experienced as positive sources of pleasure and aspiration, were now absent entirely from awareness, manifesting instead as physical symptoms or experienced as agitated psychological distress and desperation—states captured in the fiery blistering of Painting 2 and Painting 3. Later these drives were to sporadically reappear as intoxicating compulsions that would sweep over me, bringing me close to psychosis.[3] Their power had been magnified significantly, to the degree that I was unable to consciously control them. Indeed, my consciousness was often consumed by them. Because of this extreme activation of the instincts, and the weakening of my psychological defenses and sense of conscious control, I was forced to try to come to terms with and integrate the fantasies and drives welling up within me in a different way. Alchemy, I later discovered, offers detailed symbolic accounts of this very endeavor.

Essentially, alchemy, as Jung understood it, seeks to bring two different systems within the psyche—the daylight world of consciousness and the dark underworld of the archetypes and instincts—into an integrated relationship, although the initial coming together of these systems can often have volatile and disturbing consequences. In the alchemical texts, the two systems are symbolized by pairs of opposites: *Sol* and *Luna*, king and queen, and Adam and Eve. These pairs are different ways of depicting the basic duality of psychological life and the potential for the union of the separated opposites or psychic systems in a culminating synthesis of a "sacred marriage" of masculine and feminine.

Our primordial experience of the day sky and night sky, each with its own ruling light, *Sol* and *Luna*, partakes in this fundamental duality and interconnectedness of the two sides or systems of the psyche. This might be a projection of a psychological reality onto our experience of the world and the heavens, or it might point, as I believe, to an underlying identity of the physical universe and the psyche. Either way, *Sol*, the sun, represents the "masculine" spirit and the light of conscious awareness, attached to the ego; and *Luna*, the moon, symbolizes the "feminine" principle and the lesser, softer, reflective and receptive light within the darkness of the unconscious.

Figure 3. King and Queen, *Sol* and *Luna*

The king and queen were the ruling authorities of society in the monarchies of medieval and early modern Europe, in which there was an assumed connection between royalty and divinity. The monarch was seen as the representative of God. Hence it is perfectly understandable that the imagination of the alchemists would draw upon royal imagery to portray the coming together of the ruling principles of the two psychological systems, consciousness and the unconscious.

Likewise, Adam and Eve, as our primordial parents in the Judeo-Christian tradition, suggest the pregiven differentiation of the unity of life into male and female, and into all the categories of opposites, such as light and dark, good and evil, spirit and nature, reason and instinct. The painful realization of these opposites is brought about through the events of Genesis, centered on the Fall. The restoration of the paradise of non-duality symbolized by the Garden of Eden therefore requires the reunion of the separated principles in a new form of relationship.

In terms of individual experience, the separated opposites are the starting point for the alchemical transformation. The conscious ego exists as a relatively differentiated center or "complex" within the psyche, usually attuned to its higher values and guided by reason, yet in some cases perilously detached from the life of the instincts, and thus in danger of being unconsciously possessed by them. The life energy that one denies does not conveniently disappear. It must be lived and can manifest against one's will, as unconscious possession, if it is not fully expressed.

To reclaim its connection to the instincts—to the id, in Freudian terms—the ego must undergo a perilous "descent into the underworld" to confront what Freud described as a "seething cauldron of excitements,"[4] to subdue the "beast within," while the monarchical principle of consciousness is simultaneously subjected to a fiery death. This process is vividly portrayed in alchemy: Figuratively speaking, the light of consciousness, *Sol*, descends or falls into its psychic depths and background, where it has to face up to the instincts over and over again. "It is the moral task of alchemy," Jung proclaims, "to bring the feminine, maternal background of the masculine psyche, seething with passions, into harmony with the principle of the spirit—truly a labour of Hercules!"[5] *Sol* or the king, guided by the light of transcendent awareness and reason, comes into relationship with the chthonic underworld, presided over by the queen or *Luna*.

To put this another way, we might say that while part of the human psyche has risen up into a loosely enlightened state of self-reflective conscious awareness, much of it remains in the grip of the dark, binding power of the instincts. Individuation in its fullest sense, as symbolized in alchemy, is concerned with the "redemption" of the entire psyche so that it is no longer the case that the conscious part of us is at odds with our instincts and emotions. At least, this is the ideal outcome towards which individuation leads.

The conflict between reason, guided by rational judgments and moral values, and the desires, appetites, passions, fears, and other "irrational" elements of our experience is intrinsic to human nature. We struggle to honor our commitments, live up to our ethical values, to do the right thing, to remain steadfast and true to our better nature even as our feelings and urges might insistently demand other courses of action, or crave immediate satisfaction and release. To become whole entails, first of all, a recognition of the gamut of feelings and impulses that move us, and, thereafter, an integration of these feelings so that we move towards a more unified state. To be whole, the aspiration of Jungian psychology, implies that we should not be divided against ourselves—or at least not radically so.

Two processes occur simultaneously during the alchemical opus. On the one hand, the old structure of the ego, with its associated sense of identity and willpower, is progressively deconstructed and effectively "dies"—we see this in the images of the ailing, burning, drowning, dying, and dismembered king. Initially, the ego is established and supported by defenses and resistances to life, which themselves seem to arise out of fear and the urge for self-preservation. These resistances keep us psychologically separate from life, a safe distance from the turbulence of the emotions and instincts. In the course of the alchemical transformation, as I was to experience personally, resistances are first activated and accentuated, then purged and released, giving rise to the experience of a psychological death. With this death, the existential gap between the individual's consciousness and life is closed. The conscious ego and the instincts are brought together in a creative synthesis; the psyche is made more whole.

On the other hand, the alchemical opus entails facing, containing, and transforming the instincts. Often symbolically depicted by the alchemists in the form of a dragon or serpent or a self-consuming uroboros, the instincts are "contained," like the metal in the *vas alembic*, and are subject to heating, which burns off the poisonous impurities. Psychologically, as we will explore shortly, the purifying process of the burning-off of poison implies the overcoming of unconscious compulsion, a binding and blinding quality within our drives and desires. The alchemical process symbolizes the struggle to liberate ourselves from the unconscious hold of these instinctual drives and emotions.

The two processes occur together: The eradication of resistances to life and the ego's defenses permits the influx of instincts, compulsions, fears, desires, and fantasies into consciousness, where they are to be contained and transformed. Whereas the old ego ruled by repression and resistance, the alchemical opus leads to a state in which consciousness and the instincts are brought into a newly forged unified condition, symbolized by the image of the sacred marriage, known as the *hieros gamos*, or in the figure of the hermaphrodite.

Painting 1 (on page 38) suggests the descent of the solar principle into the underworld of the instinctual unconscious, and also the activation of unconscious contents, which threaten to emerge into the conscious, daylight realm above the horizon.[6] Likewise, Painting 16 (on page 100), depicts a descent into a fiery vortex of hell, with the conflagration suggesting the raging of activated instincts.

The experiences of existential crisis and the descent into the underworld are key components of the *nigredo* phase of the alchemical opus, which brings about the *mortificatio* (the death) of the king. The *nigredo*, as the alchemists experienced it, is a period of inner darkness, of

Figure 4. In the *Nigredo*

Figure 5. *Nigredo* and *Mortificatio*

"a black blacker than black,"[7] during which *Sol* or the king undergoes immense suffering and a mystic death or crucifixion comparable to what St. John of the Cross described as "the dark night of the soul." The *nigredo* brings depression and darkness, suffering and sorrow. It is a sickness unto death. The phase is symbolized, as one might imagine, by corpses, skeletons, coffins, ravens and crows, and by personified images of death itself—the *mortificatio* is at once a process and an archetypal figure. Often the death goes hand in hand with being devoured and dismembered.

At first, amidst the *nigredo*, the suffering can seem interminable, pointless, and hopeless. It is a hell of despair. One plunges into the abysmal depths of the shadow. For me, at times, it seemed as if it were impossible to feel any worse than I did. I felt as if I were drinking the bitterest dregs of life experience. Death would have been a blessing, although I also resisted

45

it and strove tirelessly to retain a small measure of control and perspective, and to keep alive the hope that one day the suffering might end.

Later, however, after I'd withstood the initial trauma of my crisis, my perspective changed. Recollecting the spiritual experiences from earlier in my life, I gradually came to see the suffering as purposive, as aspects of something like a mystic crucifixion. Mystical literature describes a period of "purification" and prolonged transformation coming after the initial "awakening of the soul."[8] I felt that I had experienced the awakening in my student years and now, it seemed to me, I found myself pulled into an underworld journey into hell and purgatory. Assagioli characterized the purification process as a journey through the "lower unconscious" in which one comes into contact with the lower urges—that is, those of a primitive nature that normally lie outside of our conscious awareness.[9] As the ego faces these urges, within the realm of the shadow, so it too is transformed. The primary agent of transformation is suffering.

In my own case, the necessity of accepting and affirming the suffering that accompanies the *nigredo* was made clear to me in the following dream:

I am standing with my wife in a hotel room in Paris. In the room above us a man and a woman are arguing. I am facing the door leading out to the corridor and read the hotel regulations posted on the door. The sign reads: "Your final journey is to affirm the suffering in life." On reading these words, I feel overcome with numinosity as I realize their great significance. Instantly, I find myself floating down the hotel corridor towards an immense bright light. I feel a tingling sensation in the top of my head, the crown chakra. I realize that if I continue towards the light I will have a spiritual illumination but my brain might explode from the intensity of the experience and there would then be no going back to life in the world. I feel panicked. I look back down the corridor and see my wife and cat waiting for me outside the hotel room. With that, I "decide" to return to them. After an inner struggle, I awake.

It was in Paris, a year or so before this dream, that I had first acutely experienced a number of disturbing symptoms of my existential crisis, including nausea and dread. "Now," I said to myself at the time, "I understand firsthand what the existential philosophers were concerned with." That these experiences were taking place in Paris, the home of Jean-Paul Sartre, seemed entirely fitting.

One night, in our Paris hotel room, I woke in the early hours, in darkness, in a claustrophobic panic, with the desperate feeling that I had to get out of the room, several floors up, even if it were by jumping out of the window. For the first time in my life, I also suffered from overwhelming vertigo. Both phobias—of being confined and the dizzying terror of height—seemed to reflect my unshakeable sense of existential entrapment.

In time, I came to view dread as a form of repressed panic that had been magnified and altered by its repression. I understood that, for me at least, dread arose as a delayed trauma from an inability to experience overwhelming panic-fear at the time it manifested. The dread became a kind of secondary trauma overlaying the first, but manifesting more slowly, in a way that I could eventually experience and come to terms with.

Dread, I came to realize, is also a consequence of the separation of ego-consciousness from the supporting flow of power from the unconscious. It often arose within me in response to the realization "I Am," in which consciousness comes to a profound awareness of its own existence. As the "I Am" awareness periodically came over me, and I became more fully conscious of myself, I would realize in that instant that there was nothing supporting my consciousness, which stood alone in the universe, existentially isolated and adrift, as if in nothingness. Although, in a different context, the "I Am" is a profound, numinous experience of the fullness of self-conscious awareness, bringing with it the sense that one has stepped into a larger mode of existence and a more total reality, its occurrence was acutely problematic for me until I was able to fully experience and thus move beyond the fear that accompanied it. Until then, it would cause me to panic at the merest glimmer of awareness of the nothingness. I could not bear to face it; I clamped down on the fear; I could not let the experience unfold.

Perhaps the existential angst of my Paris experience was reflected in the setting of the dream—in the Paris hotel room. I understood the arguing couple in the dream to refer to a higher-level dispute (i.e., taking place in the room above) between the opposites—male and female.[10] The opposites in dispute were consciousness and the unconscious, ego and shadow, reason and instinct, thought and feeling, light and dark. Rational ego-consciousness was in a stand-off with the now overwhelming power of the activated instinctual unconscious. In terms of my personal experience, I was struggling simply to keep the instincts and overwrought emotional states at bay—especially the panic-fear. But it was not a question of totally subduing or banishing the instincts, which could perhaps be achieved temporarily by repression and more splitting or could probably be brought about by antidepressant medication. Rather, what was required was a resolution of the conflict at a higher level, such that the instincts and the conscious ego would both be transformed in their realignment around the transpersonal Self.

The brightness of the enlightenment or *illuminatio* experience in the dream was in stark contrast with my dark, bleak, panic-stricken state of mind at this time. I felt as if I were staring into an abyss, and I was frequently overcome with a claustrophobic fear that seemed to extend into eternity—as well as enduring crushing pains in my body and other chronic physical symptoms. I had gone to sleep that night fearing I would not live to see the morning. I was severely afflicted by spasms in the chest, above the solar plexus, which felt to me like I was having a heart-attack, as if there were something pressing against my heart, delivering shocks. These spasms were caused, I think, by bloating and digestive problems from unconsciously gasping in too much air and they also seemed to be related to the experience of dread. Understandably, these symptoms caused me further alarm to the point that my imminent death seemed a very real prospect.

The dream thus came as a blessing. It seemed to me that I'd been through a near-death experience. I woke shaken but bathed in the afterglow of the transcendent light of spirit, and from that moment I knew for certain that this crisis was one of spiritual transition that was ultimately progressive. It convinced me beyond doubt of the spiritual nature of my suffering. I thus fiercely resisted any attempts to diagnose my condition in pathological terms and thus ultimately rejected any advice to treat it with medication.

Yet the dream did not promise any prospect of a rapid solution; on the contrary, it portended a long path of suffering and privation that unfolds to this day. The divine sanction for the suffering, however, furnished it with the meaning that has enabled me, for the most part, to affirm it as a necessary and unavoidable dimension of my fate.

Another dream around that time placed me in a parking lot, with my vehicle (a bicycle) held inside a parking space by a computerized locking system. A voice announced that the computer could be reprogrammed to release the lock and that the purpose of the entrapment was to "condition a 'yes' response." I understood that I was trapped in my life and unable to move forward so that my psyche could be reprogrammed to say "yes" to my fate, whatever that was to be. As indicated by the Paris hotel dream, I understood that I was to affirm the suffering in life and, conversely, that the suffering would condition in me the willingness to affirm.

The suffering of the alchemical phase of the *nigredo* has the effect of throwing the conscious personality into the darkness of the shadow, a theme that finds expression in the following paintings.

Painting 4. Slanting Shadow and *Nigredo* Sunset

Painting 5. Gold Pool Dripping Blood

Painting 6. Star of Illumination and Crashing Rocks

Painting 7. Tree Figure with Split Wings

Painting 4 is pervaded with nigredo *motifs: the dark setting sun, the disturbing shadow figure (leaning heavily to one side), and the black ravens hovering amidst the trees. Painting 5 shows a tree, with sprouts of green foliage on its branches, suggesting new life emerging, but being pulled back towards a dark watery pool, containing specks of light or gold, into which fall drops of blood. The picture contains multiple serpent images—a recurring theme of the entire series of paintings. Painting 6 and Painting 7 both depict the splitting or separation of the opposites indicated by the division between the mountains and in the red circular shape (like butterfly wings). Painting 6 again shows a setting sun and the human figure cast into shadow below the brightness of the star. The crashing rocks point to the collapsing structures of the ego, a process that is necessary to enable unconscious contents to emerge into consciousness. The figures in Painting 6 and Painting 7 have both adopted something like a crucifix pose. The journey from the ego to the Self during individuation can be experienced as a kind of crucifixion, symbolized by the fate of Christ and the alchemical god Mercurius, to be discussed later.*

Without any express intention on my part, these paintings gave form to a number of the processes working through me at the time, including descent and metamorphosis, the splitting of the opposites, and the collapse of the structure of my personality. Contemplating the crashing rocks in my painting, I recalled Jung's vision of boulders crashing down all around him during his own confrontation with the unconscious—an assault he was able to survive, he remarked, through sheer "brute strength" where others before him had failed.[11] The prospect of my own failure weighed heavily on my mind. I thought especially of Nietzsche's collapse into insanity and death, and I feared this fate. Among my greatest fears was being committed to a psychiatric institution. I was willing to do whatever it took to prevent that happening. I felt I simply had to survive and prevail, or at least die trying. There was a heroic element working through me, which gripped me as powerfully as the onslaught of symptoms. For the alchemists, as Jung shows, the trials and travails of the hero in myth closely mirror the fate of the king and *Sol* in alchemy.[12]

As I began Painting 4, I felt I was on the brink of madness. It was in the early months of 2003. I truly feared that I was losing my grip on reality, as panic was getting the upper hand. I felt that if I lost control, and succumbed totally to the panic, I might never recover. On this particular day, these fears were acute. As I worked on the painting, I imagined a dark pathway leading to an entrance in a cave. Upon completing it, I believed that is what I had in fact painted. But my wife pointed out to me that the dark pathway and doorway could instead be seen as the shadow of a human figure, leaning to one side in an exaggerated slant. The heavily slanting path or figure, and the leaning tree in Painting 5, seemed to me indicative of my one-sided condition—as did the image of the setting sun, with rays on only one side. In a discussion of "The Philosophical Tree" as a symbol of human psychological growth, Jung connects images of trees leaning to one side or growing back towards the ground with the psychological experience of regression.[13] The tree no longer grows up towards "spirit" (the sky) but back towards nature (the earth). That is to say, consciousness is pulled back in a regressive return to the unconscious world of instinct. The ravens, also featured in Painting 4, are the birds most associated with *nigredo*, and the mood and imagery of the painting suggested death—the death I was now experiencing.

ENDNOTES

[1] Compare to images on pages 83 and 86 in Jung's *Red Book*, which depict black and red underground contents pushing up towards the surface. See Carl Gustav Jung, *The Red Book: Liber Nous,* edited and introduced by Sonu Shamdasani, translated by Mark Kyburz, John Peck, and Sonu Shamdasani (New York: W. W. Norton & Co., 2009).

[2] In presenting these images to a class for my "Alchemy of Transformation" course at Pacifica Graduate Institute in 2019, one student (a former midwife) remarked that the lower part of the painting features an image that bears a resemblance to an umbilical cord, perhaps therefore also suggesting the theme of pregnancy or gestation.

[3] As Jung puts it, a psychosis "inundates you with uncontrollable fantasies irrupting from the unconscious" (*Mysterium Coniunctionis*, par. 756, 531).

[4] Sigmund Freud, *New Introductory Lectures on Psycho-analysis*, Standard Edition, translated by James Strachey (New York: W. W. Norton & Company, 1990), 91.

[5] Jung, *Mysterium Coniunctionis*, par. 35, 41.

[6] Mircea Eliade argues that alchemy has its origins in metallurgy. Both the alchemist and the smith work with metal ores mined from underground. By removing the ores of metal from the "womb" of the earth, the alchemist and the smith are deliberately intervening in the processes of nature, attempting to hasten the natural "incubation" period of the ores, to assist in the completion of nature's work. See Mircea Eliade, *The Forge and the Crucible*: *The Origins and Structures of Alchemy*, second edition (Chicago, IL: University of Chicago Press, 1979).

[7] Jung, *Mysterium Coniunctionis*, par. 741, 521.

[8] See Roberto Assagioli, *Transpersonal Development: The Dimension Beyond Psychosynthesis* (London: The Aquarian Press, 1991), 116–133.

Endnotes

[9] See Assagioli, *Transpersonal Development*, 122–124.

[10] Jung also discusses the motif of the "quarrelling couple," relating it to the uroboros, the self-consuming serpent or dragon. See Jung, *Mysterium Coniunctionis*, par. 404, 295–296.

[11] Jung, *Memories, Dreams, Reflections*, 201.

[12] See Jung, *Psychology and Alchemy*, pars. 437–446, 333–344.

[13] See Jung's discussion of Figures 18 and 19 in "The Philosophical Tree" in Jung, *Alchemical Studies*, pars. 323–324, 259–261.

CHAPTER IV
Mortificatio and Ego-Death

To state the obvious, it was extremely difficult, in my traumatized condition, to maintain faith that the crisis was progressive and a consequence of a spiritual transition, especially in the early phases and the darkest moments. The pressure to seek medical intervention weighed on me at such times. In the early stage of my crisis I had sought out medical help from my doctor to treat a range of symptoms. At the time, my nerves were absolutely frayed, to the point that I had become extremely sensitive to even the slightest unexpected change in my environment. I recall on one occasion my pet cat had strolled into the room with his typical smooth and slinky silent poise and I almost jumped out of my skin as if I had just been subject to a violent trauma or shock. It was as if all my defenses and filters were down, and my inner core was exposed to a world of un-predictable crashing events and penetrating noises that severely jolted me. Such was my nervous sensitivity and feelings of weakness in the body that I feared that I had suffered irreparable nerve damage from the virus I had contracted at the start of my crisis.

At the same time, I was having increasing difficulty breathing. I wondered here too about a physical cause, perhaps in my lungs, but the problem, I soon realized, lay rather in an excessive self-consciousness that was in the grip of a fearful mistrust and panic, and that simply could not accept that breathing would happen by itself. I had become so mistrustful of my body that breathing, the most natural of acts, became a conscious ordeal, with inhalation and exhalation now something I became embroiled in and struggled to control and direct rather than letting happen. I just could not get myself out of the way.

My doctor ran the usual tests, but they only proved what I suspected: there was nothing physically wrong with me—indeed, despite smoking on and off for several years, my lung function had scored off the chart in one test. Instead he prescribed some mild antidepressants, which, he assured me, were not "happy pills" but would just help to alleviate the anxiety I was feeling.

Throughout my life I have been wary of medication and resistant to it. My experiences with the medical profession were mixed, at best. For many years I would not take pain-relief tablets unless pain levels became unbearable. I was even more fiercely opposed to antidepressants. My distraught state of mind and the doctor's prescription led to a moment of critical decision: Would I go against my principles and take the medication, or would I refuse it?

Ordinarily, there would have been no decision to make: I would have rejected medication outright, without hesitation. But in my disturbed state, unable to think or feel clearly, and with people around me giving well-intentioned advice to take the medication, I was in utter turmoil as to what to do. Medication would simply give me a break from the symptoms, a rest from the psychological struggle, I was told. Finally, in a state of self-loss and panic, I relented, and took one of the tablets. That night was perhaps the worst of my life, for now I was suffering initial side effects from the medication in addition to the host of existing symptoms and fears. I could not breathe. I was holding in so much air that my stomach became dangerously bloated, which put immense pressure on my solar plexus area, causing in turn the strange jolting sensations or spasms in my heart, with an erratic heartbeat and dramatic palpitations. I felt terrorized, in a desperate panic. To make matters worse, I felt as if I had made some grave mistake, going against my principles, which added to my sense of damnation and panic. During that harrowing night I resolved that I would never take another antidepressant tablet. I would face the condition myself, even if that led to my demise and death.

The transformative crisis pushed me into psychological isolation, for no one could understand what I was going through, even if I had been able to articulate it. I felt that there were not even books I could turn to for perspective or guidance. The isolation, I came to see, was itself part of the initiation into a deeper mode of existence. I had to rely on myself—on my own capacity to survive and my inner judgment. I did know, however, of Jung's confrontation with the unconscious, and drew optimism from his successful resolution of his crisis. He had survived so perhaps I could too. I felt that if I could make it through perhaps I also would be able to help others undergoing similar experiences. Such thoughts stirred the heroic character in me, which gave me the capacity to withstand the prolonged suffering and to maintain faith that I might one day prevail.

At one point, in 2002, for the first time in my life I started seeing a psychotherapist. He lived locally in Nottingham and was all I could have wished for in a therapist. He practiced person-centered and gestalt psychotherapy but was also transpersonal in orientation and was fairly well acquainted with the work of Jung, the transpersonal theorist Ken Wilber, and others in the field. To my surprise, he was also familiar with the workings of astrology, which remained integral to my worldview.

After six or seven sessions, though, I did not feel that the therapy was helping me. In a dream at that time, I saw myself being raped by the therapist, which well portrayed the sense of unwanted invasion I was experiencing. The sessions did not seem to be addressing my condition but were instilling in me greater doubt about what was happening. The doubt was crippling, and I felt as if my identity as a person had slipped away. I did not know who I was. I had lost all capacity for trust in my feelings and judgments, needing others to direct my life. I was kept distant from myself by a layer of panic that I could not experience. This panic—or the inability to move beyond it—prevented access to my other feelings. Everything I did therefore became inauthentic. Until I could allow the panic to come to awareness and work through it, I was locked in a state of alienation and depression.

I was disturbed by the self-loss and detached from myself. In submitting to therapy I was further relinquishing what little power I had left and forsaking the possibility that I might be able to save myself and overcome my affliction. In the sessions, we explored issues from my past, which are the legitimate concern of psychotherapy, of course, and for a time I myself thought that past wounding and the emotional turmoil following my parents' divorce when I was a child might have contributed to my current predicament. Indeed, at one stage, desperate for a way out of the suffering and a return to my former confidence and competence, I tried to directly address these issues. I spent time staying with family members, occasionally opening conversations about the past. I revisited old scenes from childhood, half consciously trying to tap into a lost innocence and to recover something of the untainted quality of those years. But these efforts were fruitless. The conversations felt forced and old. The familiar scenes of my youth were no longer comforting but like an alien land that left me feeling lost and empty. It thus became a period of futile and forlorn wandering through the landscape of my past, in search of healing and a recovery of my former self but yielding only self-loss. I had changed, although I could not understand quite how or why at that time.

I contemplated the possibility that lay before me that my life would become an abject failure and that my talents and potentials would be wasted and unfulfilled. Perhaps I was destined to suffer a tragic fate or to drop out from engagement with the world in resignation and protest, taking on the role of something like a suffering poet and wandering hermit, crippled by psychological infirmity. Perhaps I would lose my grip on reality entirely and lose my sanity, having to depend on others to support me and care for me. Such fantasies could not readily be dismissed for I sensed them as very real possibilities. What saved me at the time, I think, was an abiding sense or recollection of my own worth that had nurtured me from childhood on. I felt I had much to offer, and I absolutely would not, could not, let this go to waste. I resolved inwardly, almost without articulating it in thought, that I had to get out of this state of incapacitation and to realize my potential.

In some respects I had fallen below the normal level of functioning, but in other respects the insights emerging from my crisis seemed to elevate me to the perception of great spiritual truths. I had the realization that everyone else existed in a state of gross delusion and ignorance, a world in which they belonged and were at home, but in which I was now an alien. This peculiar perception is described in various forms in Gnostic literature, mostly dating from the first to third centuries AD. The mass of humanity is portrayed as existing in the land of the dead or in a kind of existential slumber, as if asleep, or drunk and therefore blinded, in their inebriated condition, to the truth. This unshakeable perception of my otherness, of seeing into the existential delusion behind the world of appearances, added to my sense of estrangement and isolation. It took me a long time to build up confidence in my own judgment and understanding of the nature of my experience. A key element of this process was my decision to reject outside help.

I was in such an impaired state, desperate for any kind of solution, that I was willing to entertain any diagnosis and any path to recovery. However, on another level, I intuitively knew that the personal factors explored in therapy were ultimately not relevant to what I was going through. My crisis was not of a personal biographical origin. It occurred to me some time later, that, in focusing on my personal history, relationships, and psychological complexes, I was, as Joseph Campbell once put it, "standing on a whale, fishing for minnows."[1] I didn't need to "fix" myself by focusing on issues to do with my personal psychology and biography—these were merely minnows. Rather, what was happening had to do with the emergence of the Self, the whale, upon which the entire conscious personality is supported and from which it arises. I didn't need to work through complexes—or if I did this could happen en route to doing what I had to do in the world. My problems could be transcended in the realization of my spiritual calling or mission, which would bring me into close relationship with the Self. This was my guiding intuition, although it was a dim and distant voice among the chaos of my psyche at the time. I suppose I knew what I had to do, but trusting myself enough to follow this intuition was difficult indeed and entailed high risk, for it seemed like working with the therapist was the last best hope I had of help from without that could bring an end to the worst of the pathology and suffering.

The therapist was, understandably, trying to help me to rebuild myself and my life, and to come to a more secure psychological space, but this only had the effect of limiting the scope, significance, and the potential of the transformation. We discussed workable solutions, within the range of attainable possibilities in my local environment in Nottingham, including employment options to try to give me a foothold in the world and some direction. But I could not force myself into a regular job, even if it were ostensibly pleasant and amenable, or even if it were vaguely related to my interests. The aims of the therapeutic rebuilding were appropriately modest, but I felt I had this titanic daemonic energy within me that demanded of me a great fate of some kind. I was undoubtedly inflated at times, but there was also a truth behind the inflation. Jung commented that a neurosis only happens to the person of a "'higher' type" who suffers from the smallness of life, from horizons that are too narrow.[2] I needed more life, not less. I needed to embrace my fate, whatever that might be, and pursue and fulfill my dreams and grand visions for the future, not shy away from them self-protectively. I had within me a greater destiny than my sense of life possibilities or current circumstances had allowed. I sensed that I could not really begin to recover until I took steps to realize that larger destiny; and so it proved.

It also struck me that the therapist, although skilled and empathetic, did not fully understand what I was going through. How could he? After all, the crisis was unique to me. I knew, in rare moments of optimism and perspective, that this process could deliver to me original insights and direct experience of the depths of the psyche. Others might have had certain similar experiences, but no one would have traveled this particular path. I had the sense that I was the vehicle for something new, an evolutionary process taking shape through me, leading into uncharted territory. Existing truths, therapeutic modalities, and long-established spiritual paths could not help me. I had to come to my own resolution of the crisis.

I explained this intuition as best I could to my therapist, in my traumatized state, remarking that I felt I needed to put my trust in God and follow my own path. He commended me but warned that if I walked away I ran the risk of finding myself in a psychiatric institution. I knew this risk, and I feared it greatly, but I took the decision to end the brief course of therapy. I had the insistent intuition that I had to overcome the crisis myself and, despite years later becoming faculty and program chair in one of the foremost Jungian psychology programs in the world, I haven't returned to therapy since.

After much consternation and confusion, I also had to let go of my long-held assumption that Eastern approaches to spirituality represented and revealed the ultimate truth. For in the midst of my suffering I wondered whether a path of meditation or spiritual practice—perhaps Buddhism or Zen or yoga or martial arts—would free me from my suffering. I wondered whether the crisis had arisen in order to redirect me onto such a path. From my studies of Eastern religion in my late teens and early twenties, I had uncritically accepted the idea that enlightenment is the fundamental purpose of all life and that spiritual paths leading to this goal represent the greatest possibilities of human experience for those able to adeptly follow the prescribed ways and methods. As much as these ideas appealed to me and made good sense, a part of me revolted against them. The thought that the ultimate aim of life was already given, and that the sole purpose of existence was to extinguish one's selfhood and return to the Void, however blissful this state might be, was somewhat deflating. It detracted significantly from my sense of life's emerging possibility. To my surprise, as a result of my crisis I came to adopt a view more aligned with the Western spiritual tradition, with its affirmation of evolution and the value of the historical process as meaningfully directed, and the belief in the possibility of the individual making a significant, perhaps decisive, contribution to this process. The crisis was attempting to deepen rather than dissolve my sense of selfhood.

The methods of spiritual practice were also proving harmful to me. After trying to meditate to overcome my symptoms and to find a measure of peace—including concentrating on the chakras (subtle energy centers in the body) and doing visualization exercises—I would dream of being electrocuted by a young Indian man. On another occasion, in late December 2003, in a sustained act of meditative concentration I tried to overcome myself once and for all, only to dream that night that I was forcing myself under water, to the bottom of the ocean, there to drown or dissolve by extinguishing my conscious self. I could perhaps willfully do away with myself so that there was no one left to suffer, but is this what I wanted? Would this be a real solution? I felt alarmed by the dream, fearful of losing myself forever, and quickly abandoned this endeavor.

For the most part, my attempts to meditate, I eventually concluded, were not enabling me to transcend my ego but were strengthening the state of repressive control by the ego. Why did I meditate? I had no spontaneous urge to meditate; I was doing it to save myself, to flee my suffering, or because I thought one must meditate to live a spiritual life. But my own natural response to life, my inner nature, did not wish to do this or desire it. A child, absorbed in the play and wonder of life, would not meditate. Spiritual practice is a device of the ego, I thought. My mental commitment to a spiritual life and belief in the validity of a path of meditation were at odds with my authentic response to life. They were assumptions and appendages of my old ego that imagined itself to be spiritual.

In time, then, I began to inwardly challenge the idea that the aim of life was already determined and ascribed by the spiritual traditions, as if there were no new directions to discover, no new realizations to be attained. I felt resolutely that such perspectives inhibited the unfolding of my life, although it seemed to me like rank heresy to entertain this idea and to admit that conclusion to myself. I could not bear to stand alone in that realization. It felt at times as if I were being called to reject the weight of spiritual history, which I had uncritically held in such high esteem. It was extremely difficult to do this, of course; I was fearful of the implications of where it might lead me. I swung repeatedly between inflation, feeling swollen by the profound insights breaking through me, and despair and damnation, when I would be riddled with doubt and inclined to fall back on old truths and old advice.

From the onset of my crisis, the teachings and prescriptions for how to live, detailed in every spiritual or psychological book I had ever read, became like commandments, rules about how I should approach life. I felt as if I were trapped in a cage of rules, caught in a game I could not get out of. I had meddled with the occult laws of life and was now being punished for my transgression, or so it seemed. Each thought and impulse that arose in me was conditioned by or opposed by something I had read, which in turn called up another instruction, another guiding principle or "truth" to reckon with, in an endless vicious cycle of often contradictory instructions. I would think, among other things, of the teachings of Christianity and Buddhism and Taoism, and the guiding ideas propounded by Jung, Nietzsche, Joseph Campbell, Ken Wilber, and Edgar Cayce, and of every interpretation I had read of the details of my astrological chart, to the point that I was exhausted and overwhelmed, lost in utter confusion.[3] My ego was in a tangled knot. Each thread I pulled made it tighter. The entrapment inevitably evoked further panic and the fear of insanity.

The solution to my dilemma came to me slowly, after many months of suffering at the hands of my fearful, knotted ego. I first learned to deal with the panic, to "catch" it as it arose rather than blindly respond to it, and then to contain it. From there, I began to see how the particular thoughts, rules, pieces of advice, and spiritual instructions that I was so utterly overwhelmed by were all being marshaled and commanded by the old ego. That is, they arose in response to a fearful reaction to life and a desperate attempt to remain in control or to save myself. I reflected on the biblical insight that "whoever seeks to save his life will lose it" (Luke 17:33), recognizing that so much of my spiritual and psychological interests were being commanded by the egoic impulse towards self-protection and self-preservation—the desire to save my life. I realized that I did not need to respond to the rules or directives or my desperate need for answers and methods as to how I should live. Rather, I needed to become aware of how my own fearful response held me captive to these rules and ideas. I needed to break my unconscious reaction to the fear that catapulted me into my attempts at control. This was extraordinarily difficult and became possible only after a prolonged period—three years or so—of sustained sur-veillance and investigation of the motivations behind my thoughts, feelings, and reactions. I had to slow down my psychological process enough to catch fear in the act, so to speak, and then stop myself responding automatically to it. I became almost hyper-vigilant of my inner process, from waking to sleeping. If I let myself go (that is, abandon my vigilance and give in to my emotions), even for a short time, invariably I would fall under the influence of some corrupting reaction, and spiral into my usual tendency towards endless thinking through of questions about life, endless associations between different ideas and teachings—a pattern all prompted by fear, manifesting as an urge to control.

I was more readily able to maintain vigilant awareness when I withdrew from the world and did not engage socially or get involved in activities that would stir me emotionally. But one cannot exist this way at all times. As soon as I got pulled into extraverted activity or succumbed to the craving to experience again the freedoms and pleasures of life, I would, without realizing, quickly lose myself in manic excitement stirred by the taste of long-departed happiness and the prospect of release from symptoms and suffering. When this happened, I would sometimes dream of thieves, for my consciousness had effectively been stolen from me. The dream would be enough to alert me to the unconscious possession state I had fallen into.

In time, I realized through prolonged psychological hardship that I did not need to do anything to control my life. Rather, I needed to overcome the urge to control my life, and to slay the personality that had grown up around this urge. This heroic struggle was against the former heroic urge to control, attached to my ego, which had morphed into a kind of tyrant-ogre. The hero's adventure, as I have described elsewhere, is that archetypal-mythic pattern that pertains to the struggle, sacrifice, death, and rebirth of the conscious identity en route to individuation.[4]

I came to recognize that the ego-structure arises from a self-protective drive, associated with fear. In Jungian terms, the ego-structure develops in part to protect us from the painful experience of the shadow, with its acute sense of shame, inferiority, self-judgment, guilt, and so forth. The ego-structure protects us from painful experiences, but eventually it becomes the barrier to wholeness. As individuation unfolds, the persona that masks the shadow starts to dissolve and the ego fails in its adaptation to the challenge of life. The structure of the ego collapses, like a Tower of Babel destroyed by a divine thunderbolt—perhaps crashing down to earth in a shattering crisis or perhaps, for some people, dismantled brick by brick through the steadier, slower path of therapy or spiritual practice. The shadow can then be faced and integrated, as a new personality structure forms that better reflects the wholeness of the psyche.

All these developments in my inner awareness, coupled with my rejection of established teachings and outside help, pushed me further and further along my own individual path. The nature of this path is perforce solitary and isolating. I felt identified with Nietzsche in this respect, although I could not read his books during my crisis. He was too disturbing, too extreme, too willful—and I was fearful of suffering his fate and falling into manic inflation and insanity. But I had read enough of Nietzsche's work before my crisis to recognize in my own life path at that time a similar course to his own, and I felt increasingly persuaded by his revelation of a new evolutionary direction emerging in human experience, potentially birthing a new kind of being. I felt that something new was being forged within and through me. I seemed to be experiencing this somatically, through the sensation of minor explosions in my head, as if the cells in my brain were being reprogrammed. I do not know if this was the case, but the fantasy impressed itself on me and seemed to fit the experience.

I continued to process these experiences privately and mostly in secret, adapting myself to the solitary path. But I was never entirely alone in the process, unwaveringly supported by my wife especially, and by family members. Without this support I would not have lived to tell the tale. My wife was my sole connection to reality. Her steadfast love and willingness to endure my sufferings and erratic psychological shifts saved me from a fate far worse than the one I experienced.

I was also to benefit from what Joseph Campbell called "supernatural aid," in the form of a higher guidance that came to me in moments of great need in the midst of darkness.[5] Although I was consciously embroiled in virtually every instant of the transformation, acutely mindful to the point of exhaustion of every thought and changing sensation within me, I also recognized that the process was being overseen by a transcendent power beyond my reach, which I imagined and experienced as the God of my earlier spiritual experiences at university. I instinctively developed the habit of repeating to myself certain inspirational sentences from religious literature. When all seemed lost, words quoted from the Koran in Campbell's *The Hero with a Thousand Faces* would come to me: "Well able is Allah to save."[6] Although derived from a religious tradition outside of my own background, these words would resonate through me and seemed unquestionably true. If God (or Allah) could lead me into this psychological torment, He could also deliver me from it and bring it to an end at the right moment. Likewise, from Händel's *Messiah*, I would recall the line: "He trusted in God that He would deliver him; let Him deliver Him if He delight in Him" (from Matthew 27:43 and Psalm 22:8). In certain moments, Bach's *Jesu Joy of Man's Desiring* also provided a portal to spiritual experience, transcendence, and emotional release, bringing me close to God. Faith was a redeeming virtue when all other faculties and resources failed me. Faith could sustain me even through the experience of death.

In alchemy, the suffering of the *nigredo* moves one towards psychological death. Another dream served to confirm my own impending *mortificatio*:

> *I am with an old friend, Richard, from elementary (primary) school, initially in a church, then later outside sleeping under blankets. As I am lying there, I hear a voice say repeatedly: "Death is coming . . . death is coming." I am frightened and call out for help to my father and grandfather who are standing at my feet. I realize they cannot help me and am resigned to my fate. I then realize I am pregnant.*

The extent of my suffering was such that I spent almost every waking moment absorbed in the intense struggle against myself, against physical symptoms, the fear of insanity, and the prospect of death. Under this kind of unbearable pressure dream interpretation became a life-or-death issue. I felt I simply *had* to recall the details of my dreams and interpret their meaning, and I strained my faculties to do this. On this occasion, I remembered that what was unique about my friend Richard, from my elementary school, was that one day he had unexpectedly told me that the man I had believed to be his father was not in fact his real father. I therefore understood his appearance in the dream to refer to the quest

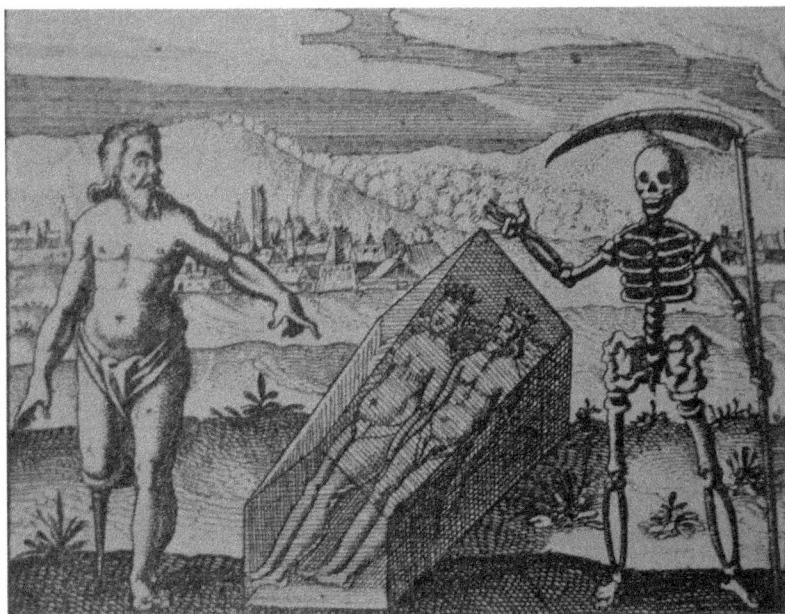

Figure 6. *Mortificatio*

Figure 7. The *Nigredo* Standing on the *Rotundum*

or journey to find out who my real father was, in the deepest sense—that is, the father principle as the guiding authority of my life. The connection to this theme is reinforced by the presence of my father and my paternal grandfather; I understood that I was to die, in a sense, to my biological lineage and also that the old ruling principle—the father principle—was the aspect of my nature, like the alchemical king, that must perish in order that I might be transformed. More specifically, the death was of my existing psychological mode of being, structured around the ruling principle of the ego. It was a death of the previous form of egoic willpower upon which the sense of "I" and the capacity for conscious thought and action were based. That ego could be considered a false ego in that it was not rooted in the deeper Self, but its experience of reality and its existence were very real and its death also very real. The aim of the transformation was not to eliminate the ego entirely, but to reform it in service of the Self.

Years earlier, while a student in Leeds, I had a dramatic dream that seemed to prophetically anticipate what was to unfold during my crisis:

I am in a dark arena or amphitheater, where events are being orchestrated by a Master of Ceremonies. The amphitheater contains a body of water within it. High up in a balcony area, I wait seated in line behind some other people from various points of my life until my name is announced. I then step forward into the arena. Responding to the call, I soon became embroiled in a fierce struggle against the Master of Ceremonies, who at that point has morphed into an evil power—a fight in which we are both pulled under water. Eventually, I gain the upper hand. The Master of Ceremonies (who now looks not unlike Emperor Ming from Flash Gordon*) shrivels up and is transfigured into a substance contained within a syringe. I understand that he has been defeated but cannot be destroyed entirely. He continues to exist in essence within the syringe and could return.*[7]

Mortificatio and Ego-Death

Almost a decade later, as I suffered at the hands of my knotted and fearful ego in the midst of my crisis, I recalled the dream of the Master of Ceremonies, who I took to be a symbolic form of the ruling principle of the ego, orchestrating the stage of life. In a flash, as the dream came to mind, I found myself confronting this figure again in a vivid vision, spontaneously delivering blow after blow as I sought to subdue him and become free. In this period of my life, I realized, I was enacting the underwater struggle, as the earlier dream had foretold. It demanded of me an almost superhuman effort. Psychological death was not something that would just happen to me of its own accord; rather, I was deeply embroiled in it, and had to struggle ceaselessly against different aspects of myself. I felt it to be a somewhat paradoxical combination of being caught up in a process beyond my control, from which I could not escape, and of having to overcome myself through my own efforts. I felt as if the process were relying on my conscious participation to make possible the ego-death.

Again, while this experience of ego-death was acutely personal to me it was also partly comprehensible in terms of the collective transition playing itself out across modern civilization. What was taking place, I believe, was the death within me of the patriarchal conditioning that has so shaped the sociology and the psychology of modern Western civilization. As Freudian psychoanalysis describes, the ego is conditioned by the superego, functioning like the hard hand of the father, ruling the house of the psyche in its enforcement of moral imperatives and laws of civilized life, which through the moral conscience shape our mode of life and ways of being in the world. The superego is the introjected morality of our experience of authority figures, espousing and perpetuating the values of the culture. This morality opposes and keeps in check the unbounded appetites of the id—the instinctual unconscious—and thus serves an essential function in enabling us to adapt to the requirements of civilized life. Like the old king in alchemy, however, the socially conditioned father principle has to be overthrown if one is to move beyond the limits of the ego and return to recover one's essential nature from the depths of the unconscious.

In my own case, the "death is coming" dream stirred in me much concern, for obviously one does not relish the prospect of one's own death. But I was encouraged that death and new life were here juxtaposed. My pregnancy in the dream, I recognized, alludes to a second, spiritual birth. It was not only death, but death as a prelude to rebirth. I had cause for optimism.

ENDNOTES

[1] Joseph Campbell, and Bill Moyers, *The Power of Myth*, 1988 (Repr., New York: Anchor Books, 1991), 46–47.

[2] As Jung puts it: "There are vast masses of the population who, despite their notorious unconsciousness, never get anywhere near a neurosis. The few who are smitten by such a fate are really persons of the 'higher' type who, for one reason or another, have remained too long on a primitive level. Their nature does not in the long run tolerate persistence in what is for them an unnatural torpor. As a result of their narrow conscious outlook and their cramped existence they save energy; bit by bit it accumulates in the unconscious and finally explodes in the form of a more or less acute neurosis." Jung, "The Relations between the Ego and the Unconscious" in *Two Essays on Analytical Psychology*, par. 291, 184.

[3] Edgar Cayce was an American psychic known as "the Sleeping Prophet" who claimed to access information in the "Akashic records"—an esoteric idea of a universal storehouse of knowledge containing records of individual past lives.

[4] See Keiron Le Grice, *The Rebirth of the Hero: Mythology as a Guide to Spiritual Transformation* (Repr., Ojai, CA: ITAS Publications, 2022).

[5] Campbell, *Hero with a Thousand Faces*, 69–77.

[6] Campbell, *Hero with a Thousand Faces*, 66.

[7] I was to meet the dark adversary in the syringe again in 2021.

CHAPTER V
Solutio and the *Prima Materia*

In 2002, I was suffering great distress from my inability to breathe naturally and from hyperventilation. Unconsciously, I was gasping in air, in near-constant imperceptible shallow breaths. My abdomen would barely twitch with each passing exhalation. Without realizing, I resisted hyperventilation but suffered strange bodily symptoms as a result, including burning sensations in my lips, jaw ache, numbness, digestive problems, migraine headaches, weakness in my arms and legs, and the sensation of explosions in my head. Most of all, though, I was crippled by not being able to let breathing happen naturally—breathing was an overly conscious ordeal.

At this time, distracting myself on a short break in London with Kathryn, I made my way into what was then Borders bookstore on Oxford Street—a large shop spread over several floors. That day, as I perused the psychology section, I pulled out a book by Czech psychiatrist Stanislav Grof, whose work I was familiar with but had not studied in any detail.[1] Almost immediately, I found myself irresistibly drawn to Grof's descriptions of the phenomenology of death-rebirth experiences manifesting through psychospiritual crises or in sessions of psychedelic therapy. He had found that these rebirth experiences closely mirror the phases of biological birth—and indeed that the two kinds of birth are overlaid such that the reliving of biological birth in a non-ordinary state of consciousness can facilitate a second spiritual birth, leading one out of the confines of the "skin-encapsulated ego."[2] As I read, I was drawn especially to Grof's description of the physical symptoms that formed part of the phenomenology of rebirth, many of which I myself had experienced. I was struck too by his focus on intentional hyper-ventilation as a method to initiate non-ordinary states of consciousness and to move through the death-rebirth process. Almost immediately, it was as if I had been given permission to hyperventilate and my fear of the consequences of hyperventilation had been partially removed. Spontaneously, a sustained period of powerful, deep breathing broke out in me there in the middle of the bookstore, bringing tremendous physical and psychological relief (I kept it hidden, as best I could). Although the relief was only temporary, it nevertheless removed my fear of hyperventilation such that I was more able and willing to let it happen in the future.

Grof's work also gave me a more explicit framework for understanding the process of psychospiritual rebirth that I was embroiled in. Yes, my experience was unique to me, and seemed to be part of an emerging evolutionary step forward in the nature of psychological experience at a collective level, as Nietzsche had described, but the process was an archetypal one, featuring discernible phases and themes common to anyone who passes through an initiatory transformation of one kind or another. Of course, it is a similar insight, I was later to discover, that is conveyed by alchemy, although different from Grofian psychology in its approach and method.

The *nigredo* phase of the alchemical opus is instigated, Jung suggests, by the "boundless concupiscence and egotism" of the king who, in his alienated state, is naturally "thirsty" for life-renewing contact with the unconscious, often symbolized by water.[3] The thirst represents desire associated with the "primitive" feeling nature, the king's unconscious shadow side, representing those feelings, affects, and desires that have not been consciously examined and differentiated—that is, carefully recognized and distinguished from consciousness. By drinking, and therefore indulging his desire nature, Jung explains, the king is then overwhelmed by an "avenging deluge" as unconscious contents (fantasies, desires, emotions, gripping ideas, and so forth) flood into consciousness—a process metaphorically portrayed as the king drowning or being swallowed by a sea monster.[4] "The king," Jung explains, "represents the domineering conscious mind which, in the course of coming to terms with the unconscious, is swallowed up by it. This brings about the *nigredo* . . . , a state of darkness that eventually leads to the renewal and rebirth of the king."[5]

Figure 8. The Drowning King

The renewal is necessary because the conscious daylight world inhabited by the king, without a life-giving connection to the unconscious world of feeling, becomes what Joseph Campbell has described as a *wasteland*—an existence that is arid, barren, inauthentic, and lifeless.[6] In this type of condition, Jung adds, "life has grown desiccated and cramped, crying out for the rediscovery of the fountainhead."[7] Once the ego and its world have crystallized into a rigid form, and are no longer renewed by a supply of life energy from the unconscious, the alchemical *putrefactio* sets in. Then the old forms begin to rot and decay as the unconscious acts to erode the life-resistant, protective structures that have been erected. To the person clinging to these obsolete structures, as I was at this time, dreams of corroding infestations by worms or insects, sent by the unconscious like Old Testament plagues, might serve to symbolize the erosion of the ego's now debilitating control.

In my case, the psychological meaning was suggested not only through such dreams but also through physical sensations and symptoms.

Sometimes I experienced a peculiar sensation of "dryness," a condition devoid of all feeling, in which every sensation would "go through me," like fingernails scraping against a blackboard, and cause me to shudder. This seemed to be related in part to an unusual electrical condition in my body. It was not uncommon at the time for me to get jolting electric shocks from static charge. I recall some shocks of such power that, when putting my hands under running water, they knocked me back across the room.

Other times, I felt like I was drowning and had lost myself completely as each part of the psyche, unrelated to all other parts, made its own claim to the exclusive control of my being. In a kind of bipolar condition, I was caught between the two opposites of extreme repression, giving rise to the dryness, and the overwhelming force of instinctual desire, manifesting as a flood.

The main consequence of the king's submersion and drowning in the waters of the unconscious is a return of the conscious ego to an "oceanic" state of undifferentiated unity. This implies that the usual sense of having a relatively clear, stable consciousness is lost, or at least severely compromised. Now one fantasy and then another washes over consciousness. In this state the capacity for reasoned decision can be inaccessible. Personal will can be rendered ineffective. As the stability of the former conscious identity dissolves, it is as if all the drives, yearnings, fears, complexes, and fantasies that comprise the contents of the unconscious psyche emerge in a chaotic flood. They arise like violent waves in the stormy sea, as the ruling ego loses its sense of command and control. It is as if the capacity for consciousness, will, directed action, and self-control, built up over many years since childhood, has all but disintegrated. What remains are the impulses that usually lurk beneath the surface of consciousness. All the contents of the psyche swim together in a primal soup—the experience of an oceanic dissolution.

In alchemy, dissolution in water enables the discovery of, or return to, the *prima materia*, the first matter, from which the alchemical gold may eventually be produced.[8] In some instances, the *prima materia* is given at the start of the work; in others, the alchemist has to search for it, for the opus can only be successful, we learn, if the operations are performed on the correct *prima materia*.

Often the *prima materia* is something that is considered to be of little worth, overlooked and cast aside. It is described as vile in appearance and likened to feces. In terms of Jungian psychology, these descriptions point to the shadow, the archetype associated with those areas of life ignored and avoided, which therefore remain weak and underdeveloped. In this psychological sense, the *prima materia* pertains to aspects of life that one has merely endured without having really faced, put up with under protest, objected to, avoided, and judged as worthless. Often we decry, judge, and dismiss these parts of life in an act of unconscious defensiveness.

In my own case, I had always lived very much in terms of my inner life—my aspirations and longings, daydreams and plans. I was also fiercely attached to my freedom and independence. To that point in life, perhaps with the exception of my university years, I had mostly merely put up with the external world. Although I had a well-developed sociable persona and enjoyed external stimulation, I was fairly introverted, happiest when in my own company, and I was often ill at ease in the context of ordinary human relationships, at least when my own interests and passions were not engaged, for then there was no flow of drive or desire to carry me along.

Prior to the onset of my crisis, my inner reality was a place of escape through fantasy and a source of inspiration from which I could then re-engage with the world in the pursuit of my desires. I liked nothing better than to put on some music and lose myself in daydreams and feelings. But the psychological splitting had put an end to that. Now my feelings and desires could not be trusted. They swept over me with demonic zeal and possessed me unconsciously, pulling me first one way and then another. With cruder emotions in the ascendancy, my true feelings were often totally buried and inaccessible. The inner world of daydream and fantasy was no longer a haven of peace but a source of panic and terror. To be alone with my thoughts, without the distraction of external life and other people, was something I now sought to avoid, for then my fears and anxieties would spiral, threatening my ability to control them, bringing the specter of insanity. It was as if the situation had been reversed, for now my only solace and support came from the outer world—from being around people, from family life and the normality of existence in that context. Rather than my instinctive nature, it was the things and relationships I had built in my life through my own efforts and intentions that I had to rely on. The shadow represents qualities and elements of experience that lie outside of the ego's sense of power and control, just as the *prima materia* is that which is discarded and reviled—the rejected cornerstone that is to become the foundation stone of a new structure of the personality. And so it was that I had to turn to something outside of the sphere of my emotions and will, outside of the dominant rule of the old king, as it were, that I could use to mediate and support my transformation. It was the area of life in which I had felt uncomfortable that now provided a crucial foundation that supported me in the midst of this period of identity transformation.

The shadow is associated too, as we have seen, with those aspects of experience that are uncivilized, bestial, compulsive, and perhaps evil—excluded from consciousness by moral repression and capable of undermining the control, authority, and rational certainty of the ego. The shadow is closely connected to the trickster archetype, which disrupts our plans, destroys self-protective strategies, and liberates us from inauthentic patterns and ways of being. In this sense the *prima materia* as shadow is presented as the neurotic symptom that impedes and disrupts consciousness, derailing our conscious intentions, preventing us from living freely and doing as we wish.

In my dissociated state, I suffered at the hands of the split-off energy that had been rendered inaccessible to consciousness and now manifested in shadow form. Psychologically, I was crippled by neurotic fears, blocks, and resistances that held me captive day and night. Physically, I experienced the split-off energy in my body, sometimes as bloating in my stomach, other times as blocks in my head or as loss of feeling in the lower leg, other times still as numbness and aching in my face, especially in my jaw and lips. Periodically, when the split-off energy drew closer to consciousness, I felt tremendous energetic tension in my body, as if the irresistible force of my instincts were pushing up against the immovable object of the shell of my ego, with its defenses and resistances. The pressure was crushing. Of course, I came to resent all these symptoms and wished only to be free of them so that I could resume my life. Yet the split-off energy, I later understood, was the *prima materia* of my alchemical transformation. The symptoms that were so despised and reviled, and excluded from consciousness, in truth represented an authentic protest by my deeper nature against the rational plan I had made for myself and the way I had been living. The energy that I could not access and express was the power that could fuel my transpersonal destiny, if only I could recover it, bring it to consciousness, and face it. The dissociated instinctual energies were the source not only of lower urges but also potentially of the Self. Nietzsche, in the figure of Zarathustra, had remarked of his own experience that "the beauty of the Superman came to me as a shadow"— and this was to prove true in my life too.[9] For the time being, though, the disruptive energy remained instinctual, and mostly inaccessible, in need of transformation and sublimation through contact with consciousness and spirit.

I tried repeatedly to will myself forward in life in the hope of becoming free of my entrapment and suffering. But my choices were not well informed, for I simply could not access my feelings. Nor was the solution to my crisis within my grasp at the time. On several occasions, the symptoms of the split-off energy stopped me from taking the wrong path in life. For example, at one point I had enrolled for a research Ph.D. at the University of Leicester (my dissertation topic was to be Romanticism and transpersonal psychology) but, when the day came to drive to campus to register and pay tuition fees, my symptoms were so bad I just could not leave the house. In the end I was forced to withdraw entirely. In total, I had enrolled, or come very close to enrolling, in six different academic or professional training programs between 2001 and 2004. But my heart was not really in any of them, and the dissociated energy, reflecting the power of my deeper being, duly saw to it that I was forced to abandon each opportunity.

On other occasions, the symptoms forced me out of inappropriate employment positions, for three or four times I had taken on jobs for which I was fundamentally ill-suited and that pushed me further away from myself, exacerbating my alienation, and ignoring what the life force in me wanted to do. The same symptoms, blocks, and psychological anxieties also prevented me from socializing or finding any release in normal human activities until I had faced up to what I had to do. To put this in terms of alchemy, I had to find a deeper foundation for my life in the *prima materia*.

My own watery dissolution, as a necessary step towards the discovery of the *prima materia*, is conveyed in Paintings 8, 9, 10, and 11. These paintings are indicative, I believe, of my entering a state of psychological fragmentation and dissolution. This is described by the alchemists as the king's return to the "dark initial state" of the "chaos," a condition in which, Jung explains, "all connections are dissolved."[10] The chaos is also described as the *massa confusa*, a condition not merely of psychological confusion but one in which all the separate parts of the psyche splinter into isolated autonomous units and enter into a warring conflict.

Painting 8. Initial State of *Solutio*

Painting 9. *Solutio* I

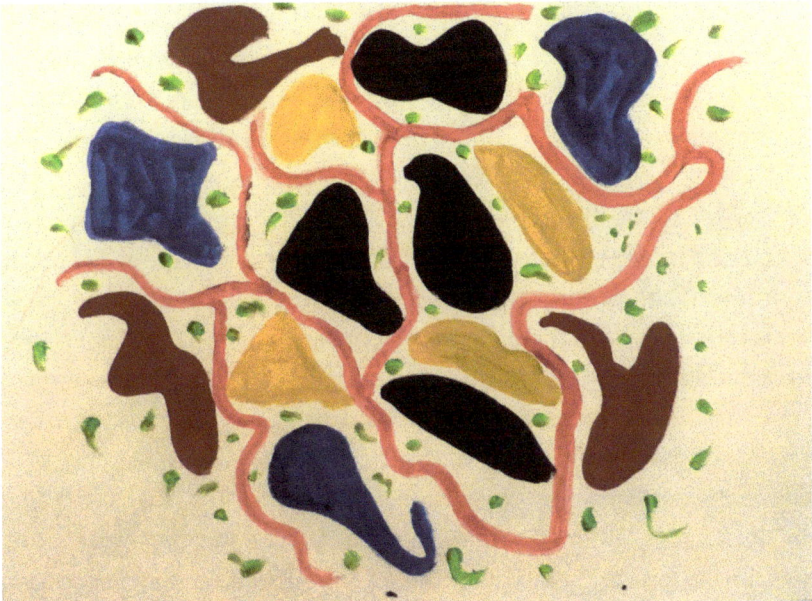

Painting 10. *Solutio* II

Painting 11. Fiery *Solutio*

Paintings 8, 9, 10, and 11 all depict the operation of solutio, *in aquatic imagery and the somewhat fluid, chaotic, and fragmented arrangements, with many contrasting colors, shapes, and patterns, seemingly without a settled order. In each, there is a suggestion of the fragmented parts dissolving and reconfiguring themselves out of the chaos of conflicting elements.*

In order to be transformed the old conscious identity has to be sacrificed and must return to the source from whence it came: "Dissolution," Jung notes, "is the prerequisite for redemption."[11] Psychologically, a state of chaos arises because the old sense of order based on the dominant rule of the ego is forsaken so that a new, deeper center might emerge and become established in relation to consciousness. In alchemical terms, what is initially solid, differentiated matter has to be transformed into a fluid, undifferentiated liquid by the process of *solutio*. The dissolved matter might then coagulate into a different form, just as the psyche continually works to reorganize itself. This process is symbolized by the alchemical operation *coagulatio*.

As each complex of locked-up emotions and fantasies is released into consciousness, so the old psychic structure that contained those energies is rendered obsolete and can then itself be destroyed and dissolved. This process releases in turn further emotions into consciousness, for the containing structures supporting the ego are built by fear and resistance, protecting us from shadow contents such as overwhelming shame and embarrassment, guilt and despair. The *solutio* of the matter is thus to be read as a metaphor for the dissolution of the crystallized form of the ego-structure that, in becoming split-off, has become insulated and detached from the flow of life energy emerging from the unconscious.

The dissolving waters that perform the *solutio* and also perform a symbolic baptism of the king are known as the *aqua permanens*, conceived as the liquid form of the philosopher's stone itself—the end product of the alchemical opus.[12] Paradoxically, then, water in alchemy is both the agent of transformation by *solutio* and at the same time the precious liquid to be extracted from matter. As the "wonderful water of transformation," [13] the *aqua permanens* is the transformative power of dissolution in the "waters" of the unconscious, and yet it also symbolizes the moisture released from the matter during the alchemical operations, a symbol of the liberated soul or slumbering spirit, emerging from its captivity in the "'chains' of Physis."[14] Put in psychological terms, through the alchemical process one is able to access the soul (the buried consciousness and feeling) that was formerly bound up in the instincts—a central aim of the individuation process, and a theme to which we will return.

Water imagery also features in Painting 12, which, of all the paintings I produced, contains the most clearly defined symbolism. In this case, I felt as if I were all adrift, at sea, being tossed around by the turbulent emotional affects and reactions breaking into consciousness. It felt too as if I had been pulled underwater. I wanted to convey these feelings in the painting.

The king's submersion in water is a version of the mythological motif of the "night-sea journey," as described by Leo Frobenius and taken up by Jung and Joseph Campbell. It is a submersion in the darkness of the water in order to find the "treasure hard to attain" and thus to be regenerated.[15] This treasure is the symbolic equivalent of the alchemical gold, the "physical goal of alchemy," which represented, Jung reports, "the panacea, the elixir of life."[16] The ego, the vessel of consciousness, signified in this painting by the ship, must either willingly descend into the realm of the unconscious or be forcibly pulled down by some denizen of the depths such as the octopus.

Painting 12. Denizen of the Depths

The conscious ego, symbolized by the boat, here caught up in a violent storm, is tossed around by the turbulent waters of the unconscious. Meanwhile, emerging unseen from below, an octopus ominously threatens to pull the boat down into the depths where lies, at the bottom of the ocean, the glistening buried treasure.

I experienced the latter. I felt that I had been pulled under water, such that the brightness and lucidity of my consciousness were gone. I was no longer free but held captive below in the depths. Very occasionally, I would catch a glimpse of light, as if I had momentarily approached the surface, reminding me of the joy of the natural psychological freedom I once had, but plunging me into resignation and sometimes despair when it passed. I knew the light was there, above the water, but I could not get to it no matter how much I strained and struggled. While I inhabited the same world, in that my external environment was the same, everything was somehow inexplicably changed. The once familiar and comforting streets and scenes around my home in Nottingham now felt like an alien landscape. I wandered adrift, with no felt connection to anything, trapped in this condition. I found the everyday world excruciatingly unbearable—dry, dead, pointless, mind-numbingly shallow and superficial. My intolerance for the everyday world was matched only by my damning judgments of the people inhabiting it. I could not bear ordinary life; to me, it was not life but death.

The loss of freedom was a cause of great distress to me. The condition felt, if not permanent, then at least of a long and unknown duration. It took me years to be sufficiently reconciled to this loss of freedom. At first, I responded instinctively to my desire to become free again. I acted on it. Later, I came to see how I unconsciously reacted to that desire. I started to see the urge to be free as something that I did not have to respond to. The yearning for freedom was fuelled in part by a panic-fear of entrapment. If I could face and accept the fear, the urge for freedom lost its power. It was in this manner that I came to terms with my impaired and trapped condition. It was the fearful ego in me that needed to be free. The larger person that I also am—the Self—could embrace both freedom and entrapment. Thus freedom came, in the end, not in the manner I thought it would, but through psychological transformation, through the experience of ego-death.

As I came to discern more fully over the years, since the time of my crisis I have found myself forced, through repeated suffering, to accept a different psychological-existential reality. My life was no longer my own, so to speak, for since then, if not before, I have had to reckon with another power directing affairs from behind the scenes that has taken away my individual freedom, at least in the manner I used to experience it. Needless to say, relinquishing the freedom to choose as I wish and to control my life as I see fit has been extremely hard to accept and accomplish. As Jung remarked, human beings tend to prefer their own will and desire to "God's secret intention" for us.[17] From the time of my crisis, "God's secret intention" has impressed itself on me and has become a dominant force in my life, forcing me to overcome my former personal will and the ego personality attached to it.

ENDNOTES

1 Stanislav Grof is the Czech psychiatrist and founder (with Anthony Sutich and Abraham Maslow) of transpersonal psychology, known for his research into "non-ordinary states of consciousness" and psychedelics as a form of experiential psychotherapy. With his late wife, Christina Grof, he developed the method of holotropic breathwork, based on intentional hyper-ventilation, to facilitate experiences of death-rebirth. Grof understands the death-rebirth process in terms of perinatal psychology, finding striking parallels between the memories of biological birth (as reported in non-ordinary states of consciousness) and experiences of psychospiritual rebirth, in that both seem to be configured according to the same stages or "Basic Perinatal Matrices." See Stanislav Grof, *The Psychology of the Future* (Albany, NY: State University of New York Press, 2000).

2 The "skin-encapsulated ego" is a term coined by Alan Watts.

3 Jung, *Mysterium Coniunctionis*, par. 365, 272.

4 Jung, *Mysterium Coniunctionis*, par. 364, 272.

5 Jung, *Psychology and Alchemy*, par. 496, 415–417.

6 See Joseph Campbell, *Creative Mythology: The Masks of God*, vol. IV (London: Arkana, 1995), part II. See also, Le Grice, *Rebirth of the Hero*, 92–95.

7 Jung, *Psychology and Alchemy*, par. 74, 60.

8 The *prima materia*, also known as the arcane substance, is literally the "first matter," signifying psychologically our essential nature to which we must return in order to be transformed. Jung describes the *prima materia* as "the mother of the lapis" (Jung, *Mysterium Coniunctionis*, par. 14, 18).

9 Nietzsche, *Thus Spoke Zarathustra*, 112.

10 Jung, *Mysterium Coniunctionis*, par. 381, 283.

[11] Jung, *Mysterium Coniunctionis*, par. 381, 283. Water, Jung notes, has a "... decomposing and dissolving property which anticipates the king's dismemberment" (*Mysterium Coniunctionis*, par. 361, 269).

[12] Jung defines the *aqua permanens* as "a ubiquitous and all-pervading essence, an *anima mundi* and the 'greatest treasure,' the innermost and most secret numinosum of man" (Jung, *Mysterium Coniunctionis*, par. 372, 278).

[13] Jung, *Mysterium Coniunctionis*, par. 372, 277.

[14] Jung, *Mysterium Coniunctionis*, par. 673, 472.

[15] Jung, *Psychology and Alchemy*, par. 442, 340.

[16] Jung, *Mysterium Coniunctionis*, par. 104, 90.

[17] Jung, cited in *Psychological Perspectives*, spring 1975, 12.

CHAPTER VI

Calcinatio and
Dionysian Dismemberment

The *mortificatio* and subsequent rebirth can be described, as we have seen, by the metaphors of drowning in a watery grave in the ocean depths, baptism, and a second birth out of the waters; but they can also be described as the consumption and purification in the flames of an underground hell or purgatory. Fire is associated with the alchemical operation *calcinatio*, which leads, if all proceeds as it must, to the *mortificatio* and a phoenix-like resurrection out of the ashes. The heating of the *prima materia* in the alchemical vessel during the process of *calcinatio* burns out impurities, destroys, and releases the "spirit" trapped in the containing structure of the matter, imagined as the release of the *aqua permanens* or as an ascending spirit, perhaps depicted in the form of white doves. Painting 13 and Painting 14 capture the essence of the *calcinatio*, *mortificatio*, and resurrection sequence.

Painting 13 was done in response to a Dionysian mood that had come over me one evening. I felt intense frustration at my entrapment and incapacitation, desperate to break free and to live again. In a surge of emotion, stirred by listening to rock music, including "Sympathy for the Devil" by the Rolling Stones (an apt choice), I hoped to overcome my suffering and blast through what was inwardly crippling me through the sheer intensity of feeling, or otherwise to totally obliterate my consciousness. My attempt did not prove successful. Feeling defeated, I produced this painting in response to the emotions stirred within me. It suggested to me not only the wild fiery flames of Dionysian passion, but also death, in the yellow and black gravestone shape and the crucifix, with the jagged red arrow at the bottom pointing down, as if to hell. I concluded

Painting 13. Dionysus Death

that this mode of Dionysian response to life had to die, that the animal power and passion in me were to be crucified. I was to experience the Dionysus motif now as dismemberment and rebirth.

In psychological terms, according to Edinger, the motif of fire signals an "inflammation by desire," the torturing flames of the frustrated or repressed instincts and desires in which the ego is consumed. Fire represents a process that both "purifies" one's motivations and effects a transformation in the psychological structure of one's being.[1] Purification may be understood here not as a process of moral improvement— although that might be a result of the transformation—but as an overcoming of the compulsive grasping that is inherent to desire.

Painting 14. Funeral Pyre

Painting 13 shows a crucifixion in a fiery grave. It depicts a tomb with a crucifix headstone and a red dagger shape extending downwards to a sharp point. The image is ablaze with the wildly burning flames of a raging fire. Painting 14 shows a human sacrifice (which I took to be me) on a funeral pyre. The conflagration is here more orderly, perhaps suggesting a greater conscious participation and cooperation with the process at this slightly later stage.

The alchemical process, at least in the form I experienced it, intensifies and accentuates the compulsion. Desires came over me with unexpected and inappropriate zeal, even desires for minor satisfactions and pleasures of the day—the enjoyment of a meal, perhaps, or going grocery shopping or leaving a situation of minor discomfort or retiring to bed. Everything became laced with a desperately grabbing or grasping quality, as if the voltage had been dramatically increased in order that the compulsive element in desire might be recognized, made conscious, and released.

The compulsion and desperation are intrinsic to desire, arising from the ego's sense of separation, or even alienation, from its ground, its roots in the instinctual world of pre-consciousness. The more distant we become from our feelings and our state of natural wholeness, the stronger desire becomes. To satisfy desire is to momentarily feel whole again, but it is a becoming whole at the level of instinct, through a reversion to instinct. Alchemy aims rather at a becoming whole at the level of the spirit. The instincts are held in check, contained in the vessel, as it were, and through this act of containment the compulsive aspect of the appetites is eventually purged.

Over the years, I developed the discipline of resisting the grasping desires as they arose, forcing myself to stand firm against the desperate pull of my emotional-instinctual nature, even as it produced prolonged discomfort. This method often entailed intense, sustained concentration on my breath, even holding my breath, as I tried to convert the automatic

Figure 9. The Afflicted King

physical response of hyperventilation and the grabbing compulsion of the impulses into feeling. I knew that I had to break the hold that desire had over me, wrestling against its binding power. From time to time, in the midst of periods of struggle, I would have the sense of emotional release at the level of the heart. I felt that I had accessed the emotion underlying the desperation, which was invariably connected to fear (and often embarrassment and shame), and in experiencing it the compulsion in the desire was overcome. I had overcome the hold of the desire and the emotion over me and taken a step on the road to freedom and wholeness.

Painting 15. Wounded Heart and Flower

Painting 15 conveys an affliction of the heart. The heart is encased in blackness and within a circle of fire, which symbolizes the transformative power of the fiery instincts in the operation calcinatio. *The heart is split open, permitting a release of emotional pain. From the open wound a solitary sunflower grows.*[2]

Fire, manifest through the process of *calcinatio*, is an altogether apt description of the burning point of the struggle. It is a metaphor, for obviously nothing is literally on fire, but in my own case I often also experienced fire directly as a physical sensation of burning in my body. It often arose, I realized, at critical moments of rebirth, when the old structure of my personality was being burnt out. Fire usually brought release. This process is described well by Stanislav Grof as "pyrocatharsis"—the experience of a "purifying and rejuvenating fire," occurring during rebirthing experiences in non-ordinary states of consciousness, when deep psychological transformation is achieved through the full experience of an emotion or drive, which enables it to be released.[3]

Invariably, the fiery rebirth experiences came only after periods of sustained struggle and suffering. I felt as if the structure of my personality was being broken apart by the unrelenting pressure of repressed and trapped instincts within me. As the structure was prized open, my inner being could move through, as if in a birth, into a fuller conscious reality. Again, I experienced this somatically. The first time I was conscious of this happening, towards the end of 2004, it was accompanied by the bizarre sensation and inner visualization of being pulled through the containing structure of the ego by the giant hand of what I can only describe as an "existential midwife." This "supernatural" intervention seemed to be necessary to introduce me to this process. Later, when I began to come to terms with what was happening to me, I was able to take matters more into my own hands. I developed the capacity to inwardly "push" consciousness between opposing forces in my head, as if I had put my head between closing elevator doors. With practice, I developed the skill of gently easing my inner being through the opening, inch by inch. This was an imaginal rendering of a somatic experience, of course, but it was altogether real. The consequence of a forced or rushed "moving-through" experience would be a crushingly painful migraine and sickness some-times unfolding over several days. Even a gentle progression, would bring headaches and sickness of a milder form. But having passed through and endured the immediate consequences, at that point the residual segment of my ego structure, now obsolete, would burn away. Then I would experience a tremendous heat in the body and the sensation of burning.

I knew at that point that another threshold of transformation was upon me and that a cycle of rebirth had been completed.

There were thousands of minor steps and decisions that led to these mini rebirth experiences—periods of psychological vigilance and control, moments of letting go and surrender, and instances of willful assertion and courage to act, each elicited by my sense of the needs of the moment. Needless to say, it took me a long time—months and years—to grasp what was happening and to begin to understand how I might overcome my affliction.

Early in my crisis, during a period of utter incapacitation, I awoke one morning unable even to open my eyes, such was the severity of the blocks in my head. As I lay in bed, I found I could barely move, nor even complete a thought. Eventually, I had to force myself in an act of will to push through the resistances and blocks. On another occasion, I remember experiencing a feeling of minor triumph on willing myself to walk a short distance through the house to the collect the mail, pushing through immense resistance and head blocks. I did not understand what was happening at the time, but in retrospect I realized that I was navigating a transition from one form of will to another. The will attached to my old ego—a kind of rational willpower—could no longer function as it once did, for that self, the person that I was, was dying. Like the king in alchemy, its powers were ailing, and thus it was no longer able to govern. In its place, however, a new will was emerging—and each instance of pushing through resistance, of taking a decision to act, marked a small yet significant step in the development of this will. The blocks and resistances were the residual structures of the shell of my old personality and former egoic will. The alchemists represented something like this transition in the symbolism of esoteric Christianity, with the old Adam making way that the new Adam, in the person of Christ, could come into being.

Pushing beyond the resistant psychological structures of my old personality would sometimes deliver me, when the moment was right, to a fresh and bright new world, as if I had moved into a truer reality beyond the veil of illusion. I vividly recall one striking episode of this kind during another short trip (periodically, I found the determination to try to participate in life as best I could, despite my condition). On this occasion, driving to Cambridge on a day trip with Kathryn in 2002, I was experiencing the familiar head blocks. But to maintain concentration on the road while driving I simply had to ignore these sensations even as the symptoms worsened. This had the effect of pushing my consciousness through the resistances and blocks that were holding me captive. The consequence was astonishing. Later that day, as we spent time taking in the sights around Cambridge, amidst my usual affliction and distress, I was suddenly overcome with a quite profound sense of the presence of God. This time my spiritual revelation was not of God as a transcendent power outside of this world, as it had been as a student in Leeds years earlier, but now as an immanent divinity manifest through and within all things. For a few moments of utter joy and incomparable bliss, it was as if I saw reality as it truly is. The grass and flowers and the sky glowed in a radiance I had never experienced—they were brighter, more vivid, more real than anything that had come before in my life. I felt immediately connected to my experience as a young child, as if there were no gap in time between my childhood and the present day. Between those times it seemed to me as if I had lived in a partial reality, in a delusion—although I did not know it until that moment. I felt God's love in everything and understood that every experience of my life, in spite of my delusion, was utterly perfect—even moments that had seemed painful or banal.

This pattern of experiences—the death of the old personality, moving through to a bright new reality in a moment of birth, and the fiery conflagration that destroys the residue of the old—has continued to this day. With each painful rebirth, I find that I am able to access a reality that is renewed, pure, and fresh, like a gently flowing, glistening stream. It is a reality that had been present all along but had been somehow veiled and buried beneath the morass of incessant thoughts, projections, and compulsions that comprise our normal experience.

Navigating the process has become a way of life. In alchemy, something of this kind is represented by the sequence of alchemical phases, symbolized by colors. The suffering and death of the *nigredo* (blackening phase) eventually yields to the bright new dawn of the whiteness of the *albedo*, which is followed in turn by a reengagement with the instincts of the body during the *rubedo* (reddening) phase. The sequence of transformations is only complete when it is made real by the *rubedo*, when consciousness comes to reengage with the instincts and drives of the body, when it returns to life and expresses again the desires and motivations that continually move us forward. As Jung explains:

> In the language of the alchemists, matter suffers until the *nigredo* disappears, when the "dawn" (*aurora*) will be announced by the peacock's tail (*cauda pavonis*), and a new day will break, the *leukosis* or *albedo*. But in this state of "whiteness" one does not *live* in the true sense of the word, it is a sort of abstract, ideal state. In order to make it come alive it must have "blood," it must have what the alchemists call the *rubedo*, the "redness" of life. Only the total experience of being can transform this ideal state of the *albedo* into a fully human mode of existence. Blood alone can reanimate a glorious state of consciousness in which the last trace of blackness is dissolved.[4]

My own experience of this process was not of a linear sequence leading to a final completion, but of cyclically repeating phases, with the reanimating power of the *rubedo* inevitably leading into another state of instinctual possession, which would in turn lead back to the *nigredo*. Struggling against the compulsion of the instincts and bearing the progressive destruction of resistances supporting the ego complex would lead again eventually to an experience of the *albedo*, and so forth. Each iteration marked, and continues to mark, a movement towards a more fully realized transformation.

As we have seen, one consequence of the collapse of the will and control of the old ego personality is that instinctual drives, fantasies, and powerful emotions, previously screened out of awareness, flood into consciousness. It is as if the protective barrier screening consciousness from the unconscious is broken apart, disintegrates, and is progressively destroyed. I remember thinking at the time that the existential gap between my consciousness and life had been closed. I could not keep life, or the flow of energies and fantasies moving through me, at arm's length. I had no psychological space to breathe; my consciousness felt engulfed, and I could not hold anything back. I would periodically dream that a gas tap had been turned on and now it could not be turned off, no matter what I did.

Without the ruling power of the ego, there is nothing to control the instincts during the transition. Fears and passions are stirred and cannot be pushed away or checked because the capacity to deny and control these drives in the customary manner has now gone. As the ego collapses, what was formerly hidden from awareness must now be faced and reckoned with. One experiences the wholeness of the powers moving through the psyche and has to find a new way to come to terms with them.

Painting 16. Fiery Vortex

The above captures the theme of descent into the abyss of the fiery vortex but also an ascent, of a phoenix-like resurrection (suggested by the red and brown shapes) out of this same maelstrom towards the star of illumination above.

As I began to study alchemy and other related perspectives towards the end of my crisis, I was better able to understand what I was going through in the context of our collective psychological evolution. The modern West, especially since the Enlightenment, has prioritized the development of consciousness, the light of reason, and "masculine" Logos and science over the irrational realm of the unconscious and the "feminine" world of Eros and the impulses of the body. Christianity has privileged the transcendent God the Father, as the ruling principle of the spirit, over the immanent realm of nature. Natural impulses rooted in the instincts came to be seen as sinful and were assigned to the Devil in outright opposition to the light and love of Christ and God in the New Testament. Thus the natural dynamisms of the body were denied and repressed. When the structures responsible for this repression—whether cultural or psychological—are removed, however, the repressed forces return with magnified power.

These repressed powers are well represented by the figure of Dionysus in Greek mythology. In *The Birth of Tragedy*, Nietzsche analyzed two aesthetic responses to life, two contrasting and often conflicting sensibilities: the Apollonian and the Dionysian. The Apollonian style of art is based on detached observation of form and appearance, with the artist standing apart from the world as observer, as exemplified by painting and sculpture, rendering the world more beautiful, masking or making palatable the horrors of existence. In the Dionysian style, one is swept up in an intoxicating rush of emotional-instinctual power, as in music, such that one's individuality is consumed and even temporarily annihilated—there is no distance between observer and observed, subject and object. An Apollonian mode of being came to dominate in the modern West, with the pervasive unconscious repression of Dionysian energies under the influence of Christian morality. "The Dionysian element," as Jung noted, "has to do with emotions and affects which have found no suitable religious outlets in the predominantly Apollonian cult and ethos of Christianity."[5] The Dionysian experience thus tends to come over us unconsciously, as an unrecognized urge for annihilation and destruction, a wild longing to escape the conventions and restrictions of civilized life in a return to our natural state. Dionysus, Jung remarked elsewhere, "is the abyss of impassioned dissolution, where all human distinctions are merged in the animal divinity of the primordial psyche—a blissful and terrible experience."[6] One feels, under the influence of this archetypal energy, that one is merging with some greater power. One is freed from the painful separation of ego-consciousness; suddenly, one's identity expands as it merges with the primordial power of all life; suddenly, one does not exist any longer as a separate individual, bringing an experience that is "blissful." All differentiated consciousness is lost, however, all individual will and capacity for intentionality and moral decision are abandoned. In this sense, the experience is "terrible."

When the principle or power symbolized by Dionysus is excluded from awareness, the energy is perforce repressed and then begins to manifest unconsciously, functioning as a split-off energy, periodically erupting in outbreaks of possession and unconscious destruction, both in individuals and across an entire culture—history attests to this. In going beyond the limits of Christianity and coming into contact with the instinctual energies of nature and the "spirit" of materiality, the alchemists were concerned with facing Dionysian power and integrating it with the transcendent spirit of Christianity. Thus the primary religious figure in alchemy, Mercurius, was at once spiritual and chthonic, Christian and pagan, god and animal. He was like Apollo and Dionysus, Christ and Devil both. The two sides of Mercurius were personified through pairs of opposites—namely, *Sol* and *Luna*, *Rex* and *Regina*, Adam and Eve—that were to be distinguished and separated, and then reunited, in the course of the alchemical opus.

In alchemy, the dark underworld of the unconscious is presided over by *Luna*, the feminine principle. Because of the one-sided dominance of rational ego-consciousness in the modern West, *Luna*—the realm of feelings, the body, nature, and the Earth—has remained largely undifferentiated and appears as the dark, unconscious realm of the instincts and desires, yet she is also the source, the matrix of all things. *Luna* is the maternal womb of being, the "belly and the womb of nature,"[7] and the "universal receptacle" from which *Sol*—the light of consciousness—emerges.[8] Jung sees a close connection between Dionysus and the realm of the mythic figure of the Great Mother. To bring consciousness into harmonious relationship with this maternal ground of being, the ego must descend into its own depths to confront and differentiate the undeveloped emotional realm. In making the descent, the ego is to suffer the fate of Dionysus in myth: dismemberment.

Historian of religion Mircea Eliade has provided plentiful evidence that the dismemberment motif is a feature of the universal, archetypal pattern of shamanism and that alchemy itself has roots in the shamanic tradition. Shamans are found in geographically separate cultures the world over; indeed, the pattern of the shamanic initiation experience seems to be shared by the entire human race, dating back as far as the time of the early cave paintings and the discovery of fire. By entering a trance state or through the spontaneous onset of a shamanic illness, the shaman undergoes a "descent into the underworld" where he or she suffers an extreme ordeal, experiencing, in an altered state of consciousness, death by dismemberment, leading to some form of rebirth. As Jung notes, the same motif is evident in many hero myths (especially those of the "mystery religions") including the myths of Osiris, Orpheus, Dionysus, Hercules, Attis, and Mithras.[9] All these are variations of the myth of the corn spirit, described in James G. Frazer's *The Golden Bough*. Like the spirit of the corn, dying each year at the autumn harvest and reborn in the spring, the hero-god undergoes rebirth, sacrificing his life that he might be made anew, reconstituted, and born again each year. In Jung's view, these mythic and symbolic accounts give form to the archetype of rebirth. They are so widespread that they "must be counted among the primary affirmations of mankind."[10] In this vein, alchemy might be seen as a symbolic system that is concerned with the articulation of the themes and dynamics of the rebirth archetype. A figure resembling a corn spirit appears in two of my own paintings, on the following page.

Painting 17. Corn Spirit Ablaze

Painting 18. Metamorphosizing Corn Spirit as Devil/Jester

The dismemberment motif is also explicit in "The Visions of Zosimos," the records of Zosimos of Panopolis, one of the earliest Greek alchemists, analyzed by Jung in *Alchemical Studies*. The visions describe in graphic detail the various forms of gruesome mutilation of a figure called Ion, the "priest of the inner sanctuaries."[12]

> I submit myself to an unendurable torment. For there came one in haste at early morning, who overpowered me, and pierced me through with the sword, and dismembered me in accordance with the rule of harmony. And he drew off the skin of my head with the sword, which he yielded with strength, and mingled the bones with the pieces of flesh, and caused them to be burned upon the fire of the art, till I perceived by the transformation of the body that I had become spirit.[13]

This text describes Ion as both the sacrificer and the sacrificed, referring to the psychological experience of having to enact and live through the transformative death described in alchemy and to give oneself to it in sacrifice. Part of one's identity—namely, the shell of the old ego—is forsaken and destroyed, but one's inner conscious identity prevails through the experience, suffers through it, and emerges anew out of the other side.

In Jungian terms, *Luna* symbolizes the anima, the archetype of life, associated with the dynamism and life urge of Eros that gives to life its animating power to motivate us, move us, and make us feel alive and vital. The anima is the inner feminine principle that connects us to the wellsprings of life. In Jungian psychology, the anima must be made conscious and differentiated if one is to come to terms with the desires and feelings of the unconscious psyche during the course of individuation.

In the following dream, the need to integrate the feminine characteristics of *Luna* is offered as the rationale for my own dismemberment:

I see myself on an operating table in a hospital surrounded by surgeons. A voice explains: "You have been badly mangled in an accident and must be reassembled with more feminine characteristics."[14]

As I reflected on the meaning of the dream, I understood the accident as the crisis of painful transformation I had become embroiled in. Psychologically I was "mangled." The unity of my sense of self and psychological experience had been lost. In no form did I experience myself as excessively masculine in my way of being or in my personality before the "accident," although for several years my interests outside of work had been largely limited to sport, with its emphasis on competition and physical battle. But I came to see how certain of my attitudes had been shaped by societal pressures to be in control and responsible, and, especially for men, to not express outwardly (or even experience inwardly) any weakness. To find my own inner strength, I had first to be willing to face my own weaker side and to accept my failings at that time to fulfill

Painting 19. Dismemberment via the *Separatio*

the traditional male role of provider or to handle the usual pressures of meeting the demands of the material world. I felt the failure acutely at first, but it was later counterbalanced by a growing sense of the import of my inner journey and the anticipated prospect of a redeeming victory over my condition further down the road.

I understood the dismemberment or "mangling" of the "masculine" ego personality as necessary to permit the emergence of the "feminine" soul from the unconscious into the foreground of my personality. My personality did not really change in terms of my interests and traits of character; the change was in the structure of the psyche rather than its content. I had become trapped in a cage of the ego. The cage had to be dismantled to make possible a recovery of the soul and the related archetypal principle of the inner child, as I will explain shortly.

I also later understood the shift from masculine to feminine more clearly in terms of a transition from *yang* to *yin*, to use the terms of Chinese philosophy. My way of meeting life had been rather willful—the imposition of a rational strategy against my feelings in an attempt to prosper, or at least survive, in the world. Henceforth, however, I realized that I had to learn to use my consciousness to overcome my egoic will. It was a struggle of self-overcoming against the false ego in order than I could recover a natural, and one might say, more feminine, way of being. Until that point, I had attempted to change my circumstances by asserting my will; thereafter, my orientation began to shift: I had to overcome the very impulse that moved me to try to control my environment and change the world to my liking. My response to the world became more aligned with the *yin* quality of accepting the challenges and restrictions imposed by circumstance rather than trying to do away with them or conquer them. The heroism, if it could be stated in mythic terms, was directed to the inner struggle against the tyrant-ogre within, a manifestation of the tyranny of the rule of the old ego, symbolized by the king in alchemy. In overcoming the tyrant or "strong man" within me, I would be free to just be, without effort and straining. There would be a dynamism in this condition of simply being (something like *wu-wei*, action through non-action, to borrow another term from Chinese philosophy), but it would arise from a will beyond that of the ego.

Figure 10. Dismemberment

It would be a spontaneous response to life, expressing the dynamism of the Self. The Kingdom of Heaven, as a Gnostic logion puts it, is like a "movement with a repose."[15] It is an effortless dynamism.

As the old ruling principle of consciousness that has supported the ego dies, so the old psychic structure is dismembered, that is, divided into separate parts. The alchemists depicted this process in the peculiar, gruesome images of a literally dismembered body. Jung understood such images psychologically, as the psyche falling apart into multiplicity and disintegration. For, initially, when the kingdom of the old ego comes to an end, the division of the kingdom results in an extreme inner turbulence and chaos. The dismembered parts of the psyche are often mutually antagonistic, warring with each other, and therefore in need of a unifying synthesis.

I found in my own life, during these years, that distinct parts of me would in turn each come to the fore and effectively take over my perceptions of the world and influence my judgments and decisions, almost hypnotically moving me in haphazard fashion in quite contradictory and conflicting life directions. One day I wanted to abandon all responsibility and commitments and hit the road, breaking out on my own, reclaiming my youth and freedom. The next day I became convinced that I should withdraw from the world into a monastic life, relinquishing worldly ambition and personal existence. At other times I felt what was needed was a forceful act of Herculean will to smash through what was holding me back. I became convinced that my environment was wrong; I would recover if I moved to another city or to another country and started life anew. Or I believed I simply needed to reactivate my former capacity to ride the wave of emotion by listening to uplifting rock music. "I am so sick and tired of suffering," a voice in me proclaimed. "To hell with it," I thought. I should just abandon myself wholly to the primal ecstasy of instinct.

Such states were as temporary as they were compelling and overwhelming. I fell chaotically and trance-like between them. The most enduring state, however, was suffering through symptoms and, in response, the relentless quest for a solution, a way out. Insights would often come over me in moments of revelation, as if the scales had fallen from my eyes. The danger then was inflation, of being seduced by the thought or the voice that told me I was having experiences and insights that singled me out as unique, with a special spiritual mission, and that I was privy to knowledge of deeper concerns of which others were totally unaware. Jung described the susceptibility to accepting such thoughts in terms of the archetypal figure of the mana personality, as in the wise old man or magician or seer. In normal conditions, one might easily dismiss these inflated ideas as and when they arise. But without a firm center, and without the grounding that comes from participation in the mundane reality of working life, the danger of inflation becomes that much greater.

Fortunately, these states were relatively short-lived. The recurrence of my usual condition of psychological impairment and suffering was enough to return my attention to the problems of simply functioning and existing.

I sometimes questioned why these experiences were happening to me. I came from the most ordinary of backgrounds, born into a family of coal miners and raised in a working-class environment, attending a modest secondary school near Mansfield, in England. From the age of nine, after my parents had separated and I lived with my mother, we had only a meager income, supported by government benefits. My horizons and expectations were fairly narrow. Growing up, I had no education in spiritual matters and no awareness of psychological concerns. My father, a salesman, had stirred in me an ambition to do well in life but this was mostly in the direction of material wellbeing rather than in spiritual matters. Before my late teenage years, I did not have access to any spiritual texts and my life was more or less entirely secular. As I questioned why I should find myself the recipient of these rather extraordinary experiences, which one simply does not hear about in the normal course of things, I was inwardly reminded that humble beginnings are no obstacle to spiritual realization. Indeed, they help to provide balance in the face of experiences that, as I recognized, could easily lead to an unhealthy grandiose inflation and misjudged sense of one's own importance.

The work of individuation demands that the archetypal plurality of the psyche be integrated into a cohesive unity by the progressive establishment of a new center—the Self—which, according to Jung, is a compensatory principle of unity that opposes the chaotic state of psychological disorder. I had no sense of this at the time, but in retrospect I came to recognize that my erratic swings between different sub-personalities and states of consciousness slowly began to lose some of their extremity. I circled around the different complexes and fantasies again and again, fortunately constrained by the limitations of my circumstance, which functioned in my life as an alchemical vessel. I was trapped in my circumstance much as the Mercurius, symbolized as a serpent or dragon, is held captive in the alembic, while being heated and transformed in the laboratory. If Mercurius escapes or is released too soon, we learn from the alchemists, he will return to his former state. In other

Figure 11. The Serpent Mercurius Consuming Itself in the Vessel

words, if we let the instincts loose, identifying with them, consenting to them, and acting them out, the energy that we might have had for transformation will be expressed instead in the satisfaction of instinct. One would fall again into a state of possession and domination by the unconscious. Gains in consciousness would be lost. Once activated, then, one needs to keep the instincts held and contained. This containment provides the motive force for the redirection of the instincts towards psychological transformation.

At some point, too, I began to see that none of the responses described above would actually deliver me to freedom. With this recognition it became easier to resist them and not to act on them. Eventually, I came to terms with my task—the task of psychological transformation, which requires a patient, steadfast, and sustained effort over years and decades. For psychological transformation is truly an opus, as demanding and unrelenting as the labor of the alchemists in their laboratories.

The crisis of transformation brought to an end the relatively simple mode of psychological functioning that, seen in retrospect, had characterized my life until that point. What emerged in its place was a radically intensified mode of consciousness, in which I became embroiled in virtually every psychic happening. Correspondingly, the crisis dramatically increased the degree of suffering I experienced. Suffering became a conscious ordeal. In dealing with my symptoms, I was no longer able to just be ill naturally, as it were, and wait to recover through rest, but illness was something I had to reckon with and wrestle with at a psychological level. The crisis marked a transition to a more complex, more arduous way of being in which the separation between the unconscious and the conscious ego, with its relatively stable sense of identity, collapsed, such that the contents of the unconscious were unleashed, pressing in on consciousness from all sides, without letting up. The only solution, in my experience at least, was to progressively, a little at a time, try to come to terms with each and every fantasy, desire, fear, and other emotional reaction as it presented itself to awareness. With each facing and overcoming of these psychic contents, a more integrated psyche began to develop, as the two systems—consciousness and the unconscious— gradually moved into a more unified condition.

As I moved towards increasing unity, dreams of dismemberment and world wars gave way to dreams of "the United Kingdom" and the "European Union," as if the unconscious were drawing on progressively larger wholes and unions in the world, relative to my own life experience, to symbolize the state of my psyche as it restructured itself. In a variant form of symbolism, I also had dreams of the English soccer teams Newcastle United, suggesting a "new" and "united" structure of being (a "castle"), and Manchester United, known in short in Britain as "Man United"—i.e., the united man. Universal themes of transformation were given form through the specific details of my life and my culture in terms that would make sense to me.

ENDNOTES

[1] As Edinger explains: "The fire for the process comes from the frustration of these instinctual desires themselves. Such an ordeal of frustrated desire is a characteristic feature of the developmental process." See *Anatomy of the Psyche,* 22.

[2] An affliction or wounding centered on the heart is also conveyed in the image on page 109 of Jung's *Red Book.*

[3] Stanislav Grof, *LSD Psychotherapy* (Alameda, CA: Hunter House, 1980), 210.

[4] Mircea Eliade's interview with C. G. Jung for *Combat* magazine, published in Paris, October 9th, 1952. A complete version of the interview is included in *C. G. Jung Speaking: Interviews and Encounters*, edited by William McGuire and R. F. C. Hull (London: Pan Books Ltd., 1980). A longer passage, including the quoted text, is in the Appendix.

[5] Jung, *Psychology and Alchemy*, par. 182, 143.

[6] Jung, *Psychology and Alchemy*, par. 118, 90.

[7] Jung, *Mysterium Coniunctionis*, par. 154, 130 (quoting Gerhard Dorn).

[8] Jung, *Mysterium Coniunctionis*, par. 154, 129.

[9] Jung mentions the examples of Osiris and Dionysus in *Mysterium Coniunctionis*, 259–260, note 5.

[10] Carl Gustav Jung, "Concerning Rebirth" in *The Archetypes and the Collective Unconscious*, volume 9, part I, of *The Collected Works of C. G. Jung*, second edition, translated by R. F. C. Hull (Princeton: Princeton University Press, 1969), par. 207, 116.

[11] Compare the jester/devil figure in these paintings with the figure in the image on page 115 of Jung's *Red Book*, noting especially the red pointed feet.

[12] Jung, *Alchemical Studies*, pars. 85–144, 59–108.

[13] Jung, *Alchemical Studies*, par. 86, 60.

[14] Jung notes that the alchemist George Ripley (1415–1490) makes a specific reference to the "mangled King." As Jung explains: "The 'mangled King' refers to Osiris, well known to the alchemists, and his dismemberment. . . . He has affinities with the 'sick' or 'imprisoned' King, the *Rex marinus* of the 'Visio Arislei'" (Jung, *Mysterium Coniunctionis*, 63, note 148).

[15] Logion 50 in Hugh McGregor Ross, *The Gospel of Thomas* (London: Watkins Publishing, 2002), 38.

CHAPTER VII
The Lion, the Child, and the Transformations of Mercurius

In my studies of alchemy over the last two decades, I have come to see how the alchemical motif of the death and dismemberment of the king has played itself out across Western civilization in the modern era. The fate of a civilization might be understood in similar terms to that of the individual, with the same transformative dynamics at work in both. The king, as ruler, can be taken as a symbol of the "ruling ideas" or values of civilization at particular times of history. The king represents what Jung calls the "conscious dominant," that is, the dominant principles shaping collective consciousness. In the modern era, in one area of life after another the old ruling principles and societal structures have been eroded, ushering in the tumultuous transformation of the late modern and postmodern age. The turbulence of our own time might be understood in part as a consequence of the dying of the old ruling ideas, the passing of the old order.

In politics, with the coming of the modern era, European monarchies were forced to give way to parliamentary government, in England with the Civil War in the seventeenth century, and later in France, with the French Revolution of 1789, in which the centuries-old *ancien régime* was violently deposed by mass uprising, the Jacobin revolutionaries, and Napoleon. The absolute rule of the king, based on an assumed direct relationship to God, the "divine right of kings" to rule, was brought to an end. As in alchemical symbolism, here quite literally the king had been deposed, with members of the ruling aristocracy beheaded at the guillotine, brutally mirroring the gruesome scenes of alchemy. Later still, the great European colonial empires of the nineteenth century tore themselves to pieces in the devastation of the First World War. The "Age of Empire," historians note, gave way to the rise of the era of the independent nation state. The empires, like the metal in the alchemist's vessel, like the individual psyche, were fragmented into pieces.

In science, similar dynamics were in evidence. At the start of the modern era, the Copernican Revolution presented a devastating challenge to the established Christian world picture, in revealing a moving Earth, orbiting the sun as a satellite, rather than a stationary Earth, placed by God at the center of Creation. From its central place in the cosmic and divine scheme of things, the Earth was effectively cast out to the periphery, as one planet among many. The view of the Earth as occupying a singularly privileged position in the universe was shown to be false.

The human being, too, was decentered in the cosmic scheme. Darwin's theory of evolution dealt a hammer blow to the centrality of "man," for no longer was the human seen as a special creature, made in the image of God the Creator, and placed by Him on Earth, but now human beings were understood in terms of the theory of natural selection. The human was not of divine origin but evolved from primates. The universe itself could be explicated in terms of the mechanical interaction of material particles and forces, with God required only as a Prime Mover, setting the universe into motion, or perhaps not required at all. Thus, in the space of a few short centuries, the settled Christian view of the world had been utterly dismantled. God was dead, as Nietzsche proclaimed; scientific discoveries had killed Him, or at least opened the Christian narrative to increasingly skeptical doubt and questioning, as secular society emerged. Thus, the ruling principle of Western religion was similarly deposed.

Meanwhile, Kant's "critical turn" had brought forth a Copernican Revolution in philosophy, as he himself described it. From Kant onwards, philosophy turned its gaze towards the mind doing the philosophizing and the epistemological limits of what could be known. Unmediated access to the true essence of things-in-themselves, the *noumena*, was in Kant's view not available to us; rather, we could experience and know only a world of appearances, of *phenomena*. Positing the existence of *a priori* categories of understanding in the human mind, Kant and the philosophy that followed repudiated an approach to metaphysics that did not adequately take into account the interpretive role of the human being. It brought about an increasing emphasis on the individual mind and its innate capacity for understanding. Existentially, Kantian metaphysics, so influential on Jung, contributed to a kind of isolation of the individual psyche, trapped in a world of appearances, epistemologically separated from objective reality. In this respect, it contributed to an emphasis on individual subjectivity that strengthened the emergence of the ego as the locus of conscious identity.

In religion, the twentieth century brought a progressive erosion of religious belief and the fragmentation of the established understanding of the world in terms of Christianity. The century's world wars served in the mind of many to confirm either the untruth or the impotence of a loving God, unable to prevent the suffering and death of untold millions and the horrors of the holocaust. Proclaiming nihilism and a radical reversal of Christian values, Nietzsche was also a mouthpiece for the return of the repressed powers of the pagan world, in his championing of the body, of instinct, of the earth as against the spirit and the soul and the afterlife—shifts that are now widely evident across modern culture.

In psychology, the emergence of Freudian psychoanalysis, with its recognition of the unconscious, further decentered the human in the scheme of things. Freud, too, likened the impact of his theory of the unconscious to the Copernican Revolution. No longer could the human being be described as "master of his own house"—no longer the king—for the rational ego was displaced as the central authority in the human psyche. The human being, he demonstrated, is moved unwittingly by powers beyond our control from the unconscious. Thus not only was the human no longer seen as central to the cosmic order, and no longer thought to be a special divinely created being, but even the basic sense of human identity and rational autonomy were challenged. The human ego was pushed to the periphery of the realm of a vast psyche, dominated by the unconscious, the source of repressed instinctual urges and complexes arising from past trauma.

As if this were not change enough, physics in the twentieth century, in the form of relativity theory and quantum mechanics, undermined even our most basic sense of inhabiting a stable physical reality. Space, time, and causality—the basic conditions of objective reality, we had assumed—were shown to be relative to the observer and thus not unchanging absolutes. What seems to us to be solid matter, comprising atomic particles, now appears at the subatomic level as energy, revealing a world in which all seemingly separate objects and forces are part of interpenetrating fields of energy and in which electrons, far apart in space, may be connected to each other in what Einstein described as "spooky actions at a distance."[1]

In this spirit, too, postmodernism led to the questioning of the basic possibility of objective truth. All truth is interpretation, it was argued, following Nietzsche. The postmodern attitude is informed by an "incredulity towards metanarratives," as Jacques Lyotard put it, and an outright rejection of the possibility of an objectively valid worldview or framework of objective moral values.[2] The human exists in a postmodern flux of relative viewpoints and interpretations with none more substantially valid than any other.

Many of these changes were anticipated or reflected in the arts. One has only to compare the realism of, say, a Constable, in the first half of the nineteenth century, with the abstract distortions of a Picasso, one hundred years later or less, to get a vivid sense of the quite astonishing transformation in the perception and experience of reality that had unfolded in this relatively short space of time.

Thus, in the wake of these dramatic shifts, the individual today inhabits a world in which old certainties and ruling structures have crumbled and dissolved, supporting metaphysical frameworks have been destroyed, moral values and religious aims have been called into question and rejected, and existential truths and even the basic sense of what reality is have been undermined. Considering these factors together it is not difficult to appreciate their tremendous impact on the psychology of the individual. For when worldviews collapse, so the psychological structures of the ego, tied to this worldview, also begin to crumble.

These factors were not in the foreground of my mind at the time of my crisis, of course, but my own situation, I later came to appreciate, was partly a symptomatic expression of this far-reaching collective transition. With the disintegration of any kind of stable worldview, and in a secular materialistic climate in which spiritual experiences go unrecognized, are dismissed, or are treated as forms of pathology, there was nothing outside of myself I could rely on. I had to go through the crisis of transition until a new order came forth within me. In psychological terms, the new order lies outside of any theory or worldview, and outside of the turbulence of the emotional-instinctual sphere. It is an order organized around the Self, symbolized by the precious stone or jewel to be attained from the underworld encounter or the voyage into the ocean depths of the unconscious.

Painting 20. Diamond Head, Steps, and Volcano

Between two ice-capped mountains, as rocks fall, crashing to the ground, a volcano releases a raging fire. Below, in the depths, a serpent guards the buried treasure. A human figure, with a head like a diamond, burns in the flames and under the volcanic pressure begins to metamorphosize (as suggested by the wings). The human figure stands at the pinnacle of a series of steps leading up the volcano.

In the descriptions and images of alchemy, one gets the sense of a psychic structure centered on the Self being forged, by the fire of suffering, through the sustained extremity of transformative pressure—themes suggested in Painting 20.

Figure 12. The Mountain of the Adepts

I was intrigued to discover later, in reading Jung's analysis of the Zosimos text in *Alchemical Studies*, that, as in the above painting, the priest Ion makes an ascent and descent along a series of steps.

I saw a sacrificer standing before me, high up on an altar, which was in the shape of a bowl. There were fifteen steps leading up to the altar. And the priest stood there, and I heard a voice from above saying to me: "I have performed the act of descending the fifteen steps into the darkness, and ascending the steps into the light. And he who renews me is the sacrificer, by casting away the grossness of the body; and by compelling necessity I am sanctified as a priest and now stand in perfection as a spirit."[3]

In Painting 20, the serpent, like Ion, can be seen as the cause of the transformative volcanic fire and that which is itself being transformed. In alchemical symbolism it represents the god Mercurius who, as a personification of the unconscious, is the central figure in the entire alchemical drama. As Jung explains, Mercurius is both the subject and object of the alchemical work. The juxtaposition of the serpent and the gold at the base of the volcano represents Mercurius as both the source and the goal of the opus. Through the arduous task of the overcoming of unconscious compulsion the serpent is to be transformed into the *lapis philosophorum*—the philosopher's stone, the glorious culmination of the alchemical process—also symbolized here by the diamond-head.

In his extensive discussions of Mercurius scattered through his three volumes on alchemy, Jung provides many further synonyms and associations. Mercurius is the king's instinctual animal side, the "primordial animality"[4] that is encountered in the descent into the realm of the unconscious and is the power, therefore, that darkens the sun and produces the *sol niger*—the black sun in the earth.[5] Mercurius is also related to the anima, which, like the alchemical *Luna*, is to be transformed through its differentiation in the light of consciousness.[6] He is also described as a "the Son of God," "the Holy Spirit," and "the Anthropos" thereby establishing his affinity with Christ.[7] He is morally ambivalent, bright and dark, male and female, and is "beyond good and evil"[8] as he represents the unconscious where such moral categories do not apply. Mercurius is the *spiritus vegetavius*, the chthonic living spirit in matter, "the partly material, partly immaterial spirit that penetrates and sustains all

Figure 13. Mercurius as Unification of the Opposites

things,"[9] and yet, paradoxically, the spirit which keeps the soul imprisoned therein.[10] And he is the *unus mundus*—the "original, non-differentiated unity of the world or of Being," residing within us as a latent unconscious wholeness.[11] As all these examples make clear, Mercurius is a symbol that embraces and reconciles all pairs of opposites.

As a god and the savior figure in alchemy, Mercurius represents a macrocosmic principle manifest within the microcosm of the individual human being. This idea is suggested by Painting 21. I felt that what I was experiencing was of significance not only for me personally but also collectively, although in the turmoil and pain of my crisis this was no more than a dim, unsubstantiated intuition. I felt burdened, as if carrying the weight of the world on my shoulders, like Atlas—a feeling translated into the images of Painting 21, showing the world, held up by a man, and circumscribed by what might be seen as the cosmic serpent Mercurius. Alongside the personal individual dimension of alchemy, there is also a cosmological element to it in the idea that nature is being redeemed by

Painting 21. Atlas and the Macrocosmic Mercurius

the alchemist's endeavors in the laboratory—the alchemist is working not just for himself but on behalf of the cosmos. He is the *filius macrocosmi*, the son of the macrocosm. The alchemical opus pertains both to the process of individuation and to the salvation of the world, of nature, of the cosmos.

Looking back from a place of greater perspective and understanding years later, and informed by the experiences and dialogues in Jung's *Red Book*, I arrived at greater insight into what I had been through and continue to process to this day. What I sorely lacked at the time was the support that this kind of larger framework of understanding might have offered in helping to legitimize in my own mind what was taking place. Jung found such a framework in alchemy, one that mirrored his own creative crisis.

At the time, I knew only that I was passing through an experience that was extraordinarily rare. Even in the transpersonal and depth psychology books I had read up to that point, I did not find accounts of experiences quite like my own and able to do justice to what I was going through, except perhaps in certain passages of mystical literature. My recollection of Jung's confrontation with the unconscious remained my main and often my only guiding star.

The solitary nature of my experience—the fact that I did not have external reference points—made it more difficult to bear, but it forced me to develop the capacity to stand alone and trust in my own judgment. In moments of uplift and inflation, I felt charged with a world-historic destiny, which stirred in me a heroism that enabled me to endure and persevere through the suffering and maintain faith in a positive outcome.

At times, it was difficult to reconcile my inner sense of the spiritual import of what I was passing through with the humbling, restrictive reality of my immediate circumstances and my abject failure to meet the ordinary demands of life. My inability to remain in several modest low-paid jobs, which I had reluctantly taken on in the hope of returning to the world and contributing to the household income, left me feeling nauseously sick and defeated, until I finally resolved not to pursue this path any longer. The contrast between the profundity of my spiritual insights and the worldly reality of my existence could scarcely have been greater.

By the autumn of 2003, having sold our house in Nottingham, Kathryn and I were living with her parents in a small village in Gower in South Wales. There, at that time, I existed as no one in particular. The few people who knew me would have seen only a sick and withdrawn individual, without employment, and barely able to function in the world. No one around would have understood what I was going through. In terms of my worldly status I felt I could not fall much lower. At that point, I had absolutely nothing concrete to support my inner assessment of the profundity of my revelation. On the contrary: I had to endure and accept the humbling experience of being reduced to naught, while maintaining a faith in the validity of what I was going through and its potential value to me, in my own life, and perhaps to the wider world. Until I could prove this, I knew there was no point in trying to articulate and explain my insights. If I had shared more than the bare details of my condition, people might well have concluded that I was severely mentally unstable and pathologically ill, subject to some gross delusions of grandeur and a psychotic detachment from reality. I knew I had to let my future actions and life achievements speak for me in the fullness of time. Until then I had the wherewithal not to cast my pearls before swine or even before sympathetic ears. My primary task, as I now understand it, was solitary and deeply inward. Before I could move forward in my life, I had to come to terms with the power represented by Mercurius.

The transformation of the serpent Mercurius is further portrayed in the following painting.

Painting 22. Alembic *Calcinatio*

Inside a containing vessel planted in the depths of an ocean, a luminous yellow coiled serpent is surrounded by flames, engulfing a disappearing human figure, releasing black smoke into the sky. Hot, black coals beneath the ocean fuel the process, which is witnessed by a refulgent sun whose rays permeate the fiery transformation below. To one side, a solitary yellow flower stands on a cliff.

Only when I discovered and studied alchemy, as my crisis drew to a close, did I identify the clear alchemical imagery in this painting. Then I immediately recognized that the image depicted in the painting has obvious parallels with the alchemical *vas alembic*, the vessel, in which the various transformative *operatio* were performed on the *prima materia*. The alembic functions as a kind of uterus of spiritual rebirth, as Jung points out; it is a vessel of transformation in which, through heating, poisonous impurities are eliminated and the *aqua permanens* is extracted through the process of *evaporatio*. "Through the incubation [in the vessel] the snake-like content is vapourized, literally 'sublimated,'" Jung notes in a commentary on an alchemical text, "which amounts to saying that it is recognized and made an object of conscious discrimination."[12]

The poisonous element within Mercurius, within the metal in the *vas alembic*, is represented by sulphur (perhaps suggested by the yellow color of the serpent in Painting 22), which, Jung explains, is understood by the alchemists to constitute "the inner fire"[13] to be found "in the depths of the nature of Mercurius."[14] Sulphur is the fiery, combustible element that, as a symbolic expression of our instinctually rooted desire, is present as a dynamic motive force in human experience and thus essential to it.

Yet as the "hot, daemonic principle of life,"[15] sulphur is envisaged as a poisonous substance that has the power to "corrupt" and to "blacken the sun."[16] As the fire of Mercurius, Jung therefore sees sulphur as corresponding to the "unconscious dynamism" and "compulsion" that thwart the conscious will and thus force the conscious ego to turn its attention to the unconscious.[17] In this way, through its seemingly negative influence, sulphur is responsible for bringing about an expansion of consciousness, justifying its supposed identity with Lucifer, "the bringer of light."[18]

The alchemists believed, then, that sulphur represents the power of compulsion to blind us, to bind us, to take away our freedom. In this respect, it is connected to what the Hermetic philosophers and Gnostics called *Heimarmene*—the inborn bill of fate that holds us imprisoned.[19] Until we have come to terms with our desires and their motivations, we are not free, but dominated by a power outside of our conscious will, held captive by our instincts much as the medieval mind thought we were prisoners of fate. Achieving freedom from the power of compulsion is an essential element of individuation. To individuate, we must be able and willing to consciously choose to serve the Self rather than other impulses that come over us and hold us captive. The burning away of sulphur portrays the process by which the grabbing, compulsive element of desire is overcome. This is essential to the process by which "spirit" is liberated from matter—that is, consciousness is freed from its domination by instinct.

The serpent, pictured coiled at the bottom of the vessel in Painting 22 and featured in other paintings, such as Painting 20 and Painting 24, is one among many theriomorphic symbols of the transformation of Mercurius that emerge during the alchemical opus. As Jung explains:

> The union of consciousness (Sol) with its feminine counterpart the unconscious (Luna) has undesirable results to begin with: it produces poisonous animals such as the dragon, serpent, scorpion, basilisk, and toad; then the lion, bear, wolf, dog, and finally the eagle and the raven. The first to appear are the cold-blooded animals, then the warm-blooded predators, and lastly birds of prey or ill-omened scavengers.[20]

The animal symbols, we read in Jung's analysis, represent the "dangerous preliminary stages" of the encounter with the unconscious.[21] The sequence of transformations into different animal forms reveals increasing degrees of conscious differentiation of the anima. My own dreams featuring therio-morphic symbolism followed a similar developmental progression. At first, the animals were of a decidedly primitive nature, as in the following dream:

> I am outside on "Church Street" in my childhood hometown. I am trying to repair an old gas cooker, first with the help of my father and then later my father-in-law. We are not successful and there is a danger the cooker may explode as the gas supply cannot be turned off. Later, the cooker has become a boiler. It is now above a bathtub in my house. The boiler processes feces and waste and has pipes like bowels. Out of a burst pipe emerges a phallic-headed monster that looks like a hybrid of a snake and a rhinoceros. It climbs out of the bath and towards me. I try to kick it away nonchalantly with a flick of my foot.[22]

The setting on Church Street perhaps alludes to the religious context of the dream. As in the earlier dream in which I was dying and pregnant, here too the presence of my father and father-in-law suggests the theme of patriarchy or an expression of the father archetype representing established values and the principle of spirit and reason. The dream seemed to be telling me that the old "masculine" ways of tackling the realm of the instincts and unconscious affect were not successful. The old systems could not be repaired and something elemental and bestial was pressing to emerge.

Both my father (in his later years) and father-in-law were spiritually inclined and informed men, in different ways, and therefore their advice and the examples of their own lives were not easy for me to reject or move beyond. Both represented in my mind a combination of responsible values, will, and a degree of wisdom born of age, insight, and experience. If anyone

Figure 14. The King in the Sweat Bath

could guide me through this period, it was surely them. I was looking for answers, solutions to my plight. I wanted instructions as to how to live for I was riddled with doubts and anxieties, and emotionally all at sea. Before long, however, I came to see that in my situation all advice was bad advice. My life required a solution on its own terms. I had to find my own way.

In the dream, the cooker and the boiler can be seen to relate to the alchemical transformation by fire and water. They might be understood as modern variants of the alchemical motif of the king's "sweat bath." The

Figure 15. Saturn in the Sweat Bath

monstrous beast emerges out the discarded waste products, which is equivalent to saying that the work of transformation must be performed on the unwanted, discarded, and despised aspects of the personality—contents of the psyche that, because of their incompatibility with the conscious values of the ego, are rendered unconscious and form the shadow personality. The shadow is not wholly negative, however, for it contains within it a powerful yet rather primitive source of life energy and dynamism, here represented by the phallic-headed monster, a symbol of instinct *par excellence*. In alchemy, recall that the *prima materia* is, as Edinger puts it, "vile in outer appearance and therefore despised, rejected, and thrown on the dung heap."[23]

My response in the dream to the approach of the monster demonstrates my own rather flippant and perhaps naïve attitude towards the work of individuation at this time. After I'd left my employment in computing, the only form of social activity in my life, virtually my only connection with the outside world, was playing soccer each week with former work colleagues—until I was forced before long to stop this too. Playing soccer was hardly enough to give expression to the formidable instinctual energies that had been stirred within me—I could not simply kick the beast of the depths to the side like I might a soccer ball. Jung made the point that one cannot redirect libido to where one would like it to go, into convenient channels of expression, simply to discharge the energy. The libido has its own aims, its own direction, which the conscious ego must come to terms with, or it risks being destroyed by the unexpressed instinctual power.

As I continued to wrestle with the tremendous energies and tensions within me, the primitive animal dream image was transmuted into other forms, as in the following dream:

> I see myself as a child hanging by a rope with the noose around my neck. It is not clear, however, if I am a boy or a girl and in fact appear to be neither. I am suffering valiantly in silence when I am attacked by a wolf or a savage wild dog which becomes a lion. I realize that the child, to protect itself, would have to kill the lion.[24]

Figure 16. The Wolf as *Prima Materia* Devouring the Dead King

Figure 17. Medieval Version of a Wild Man

The wolf or wild dog is a theriomorphic expression of the ego's desire nature, a part of the psyche that, as portrayed in this dream, threatens to savage the long-suffering inner child, hanging in suspended animation yet destined to become established as the new center of the personality. The killing of the wolf/lion by the child, however improbable this seems in reality, suggested to me the psychological primacy of the child principle over the instincts—that the inner human child must be preserved by the psyche at all costs even if this means the loss of the power of the instincts, implied by the animal's death. The psyche prioritizes the preservation of the child and will bring forth its own defenses to protect the child from mortal wounding, even if this means the vitalizing power of instinctual energies must be forsaken and remain unintegrated or even permanently suppressed.

The child symbol had presented itself to me before in the following dream:

> After descending into an underground cellar, which is also a kind of museum, I am greeted by an old British comedian from the 1970s and 1980s (Ronnie Barker), dressed as a police detective, with beige raincoat, a moustache, and a hat. He leads me through the cellar to a door in the back wall. I open the door to reveal a jungle landscape. A wild boy appears before me, dirty and unkempt in appearance, like Mowgli from Rudyard Kipling's The Jungle Book. I know that the boy is me, the child me, who has been lost and abandoned for many years, living in the wilds, but now returning to be reintegrated into my conscious personality. As the boy returns to the jungle, I turn to leave. Ronnie Barker winks at me, and I somehow know then that he is a guide to the underworld.

Meeting the child in the dream was a moving and poignant experience.

But, how, I was left to wonder, could the child and the lion be reconciled without damage to either? Like the wolf, the lion, according to Jung, represents "the king in his theriomorphic form . . . as he appears in his unconscious state."[25] It symbolizes "passionate emotionality," the ego's power drive, and, in particular, its susceptibility to pride and to inflation or unconscious possession.[26] I came to realize, from firsthand experience, that it is of paramount importance to handle this power carefully if one is to protect the inner child and preserve the precious gift of conscious individuality amidst the titanic forces and alluring fantasies emerging from the unconscious. To this end the following dream was highly instructive:

> I am traveling in the carriage of a train and have the responsibility
> of looking after a lion because the usual lion handler is absent.
> Initially, I tightly bind the lion's jaws to keep it under control but I
> quickly realize that the lion can't breathe and is suffocating. Then, I
> release the lion and let it roam around the carriage but it soon
> threatens to attack and kill my pet cat who is also there. Other
> people have to help out. They anesthetize the lion and it dies. I
> become very troubled. I then see a replay of the scene in a parallel
> carriage. On this occasion, the lion-handler, a woman, is present
> and she maintains control of the lion by feeding it fish.

Around the time of this dream I was struggling unsuccessfully to find a way to control my emotions, fears, and desires without succumbing either to outright repression or to total collapse and abandonment to the instincts (suggested by the first two approaches in the dream). Binding the jaws of the lion too tightly was tantamount to an excessive control and repression of the instincts; letting the lion roam free suggested an uncritical consent to my impulses and desires, which would then gain the upper hand over consciousness and threaten the security of the inner child, symbolized here by my pet cat. The intervention of other people, who inject the anesthetic, portrays, I believe, what would happen if my instincts got out of control. I would be forced to rely on outside help and medical suppression, bringing a loss of instinct (the death of the lion) and with it, I knew, the loss of the vital energy essential for my life purpose.

Figure 18. Green Lion Devouring the Sun

The replay of the scenes of the dream in the second carriage, this time with the lion handler present, was effectively a demonstration of a way in which the lion might be successfully tamed, without harm and without danger. It seemed significant to me that the lion handler was female. I immediately thought of the anima, the archetype associated with the inner feminine principle in the male psyche, according to classical Jungian theory. By becoming acquainted with the anima, by differentiating this archetype, distinguishing the pull of the anima and its feelings and desires from one's consciousness, one could find a way to feel into the motivations underlying these instinctually empowered desires. The instincts could be controlled and integrated through the differentiation of one's feeling nature rather than denied through rational suppression or unconscious repression. It was ineffectual, I discovered, to wrestle with the instincts and insist on the rightness and primacy of a reasonable course of action. One cannot rationalize emotional affects and instinctual responses away, for they are often impervious to reason and stronger than personal willpower. Rather, one must cultivate the ability to allow these emotions and drives to come to consciousness. Then they might be experienced, contained, and worked with at the level of feeling.

In my associations with the dream image, I also thought of the lion in Nietzsche's parable "On the Three Metamorphoses of the Spirit" in *Thus Spoke Zarathustra*. Here the lion represents the instinctually empowered individualism of the ego, able to oppose and throw off the "values of a thousand years" in its confrontation with the fearsome dragon called "Thou Shalt." Nietzsche's lion symbolizes the capacity of the individual to overthrow social expectation and conditioning, and thus to win through to authentic individual experience. The lion roars a "sacred no" in its fervent rejection of the ways imposed on us by the assimilation of societal values and ideas, and the weight of moral and religious history.[27] I had passed through a period like this in my own life, albeit in faltering steps. The lion stirred within me and passionately fuelled my yearning for a fuller life, outside the patterns of conventional existence. It had driven me away from society onto my own path, but, having delivered me to this "freedom," how now might the raging lion itself be contained and transformed?

The dream image of feeding fish to the lion, I surmised, suggested a "Christianization" of instinct, for the fish is the primary symbol of Christ, the fisher of men. This process I understood to be a sublimation of instinct such that the energy within it could be harnessed and directed in the pursuit of spiritually informed life aims. For me, this sublimation was to become possible in fall 2004, resulting in the realization of my long-held aspiration to move to San Francisco for graduate studies.

Although I did not grasp this at the time, I realize, looking back now, that when I moved to San Francisco I was, on the one hand, acting on my spiritual calling to take steps to forge a life path in the area of depth and transpersonal psychology. I was living according to my highest possibility and vision for what I might become and contribute to the world, and acting on what I had really wanted to do for many years. At the same time, the "lower" drives within me—craving freedom, adventure, excitement, and pleasure—were also able to find fulfillment, not in isolation, for themselves, but in the course of pursuing my higher goal. There was adventure enough and freedom enough in moving to California to start a new life. I did not need to pursue these things as ends in themselves. It was in this way that the instincts were brought under the direction of higher spiritual values and aims. I did not clearly understand this until some years later, but I found myself intuitively drawn in a direction that would permit the kind of Christianization or spiritualization of instinct suggested by the dream.

Figure 19. *La Force* (Strength), Marseilles Tarot Card

Figure 20. Strength, Rider-Waite Tarot Card

These insights, which came to me after repeated failings and struggles over a period of many months and years, were extremely difficult to put into practice. At every step I had to struggle to master the emotions and drives moving through me, to ensure my consciousness could remain in control. Yet I felt sure I was proceeding along the right lines, for my lion-handler dream and the interpretation I gave to it were reinforced by a startling synchronicity in 2003.

Before another brief trip to London, I had a vivid dream:

I find myself participating in a kind of board game, which is not positioned horizontally, lying flat on a table, but vertically as if I am seeing it square on, while standing. I then actually enter into

139

the game myself, moving around the board, which I realize is like a street map of London, featuring major landmarks (though it was more like Snakes and Ladders than Monopoly). Within the game, I find myself pursued across London by a bearded Rastafarian man, chasing me from street to street, as I ran breathlessly. For some reason, I have possession of his hamster, and he is trying to retrieve it.

On waking, I was immediately impressed by the rather unusual nature of the dream. Thereafter, however, for several days I did not stop to think of it again.

Arriving in London, a week or so after the dream, I paid a visit to Watkins Books near Leicester Square, as was my habit. The shop specializes in mind-body-spirit titles, from Jungian psychology and esoteric subjects to books on healing and consciousness. On the lower level of the store, to the far-left corner of the back wall, there is a section on esoteric religion. As I made my way towards that area, to my surprise I caught sight of a man, bearded and in Rastafarian garb, perusing the books. As I looked more closely, I knew that it was the same man from my dream, which then flashed through my mind. By way of context I should point out that I have never before or since seen a Rastafarian in Watkins. The improbability of this occurrence and the uncanny connection to the figure in my dream left me dumbstruck. I always pay close attention to synchronicities (and at the time they were frequent occurrences) so I decided I should discreetly observe the man in case anything significant might happen. A short time later, as he left the store, I could see he had been browsing books on Gnosticism. I made my way over to that section and immediately pulled a book from the shelf. It was a translation of the Gospel of Thomas, the Gnostic text unearthed from the desert sands in Nag Hammadi, Egypt in 1945. The text, I was to discover, is comprised of a collection of sayings attributed to Jesus, bearing considerable similarity to many of the teachings in the synoptic gospels, and especially the so-called Q gospel (from the German *Quelle* meaning source), which forms the core of the gospels of Mark, Matthew, and Luke but does not contain any narrative of the life of Jesus or accounts of miracles or the moral prohibitions we find in the books of the New Testament. The Gospel of Thomas was to have a dramatic influence on me.

Somehow, through the strange correspondence between the dream and the events in the bookstore, I had been led synchronistically to this text, which immediately became an invaluable source of guidance as I navigated my transformative crisis. The *logia*, or sayings, spoke to me in all their psychospiritual depth, offering insights that pertain to the same process of transformation that was the concern of the alchemists. Looking back now, it seems to me quite remarkable, even astonishing, that the dream and synchronicity should conspire in this way to bring me to the very book I needed to work through my crisis.

Logion 7, featuring the lion symbol, was especially instructive in the context of my dream of the lion in the train carriage:

Jesus said:
Happy is the lion which the man will eat,
and the lion will become man;
and abominated is the man whom the lion will eat,
and the lion will become man.[28]

Applying this to my own experience, I realized that I must find a way to express the power of the instinctual unconscious (eat the lion) or this power would possess me unconsciously (eaten by the lion). The latter eventuality, I understood, could turn one into an abomination through the loss of human moral values, human feeling, and the capacity for conscious discrimination. Or it could destroy one entirely. Another logion offers a similar warning: "If you bring forth what is within you, what is within you will save you. If you do not bring forth what is within you, what you do not bring forth will destroy you."[29] By human standards, such a spiritual or psychological law seems harsh indeed: realize yourself or be destroyed. But essentially these *logia* imply that one has to find a way to live the vital drive and daemonic energy inherent to one's nature. To live in disregard or denial of one's daemon will ultimately be self-defeating. For the energies that one could or should be expressing do not simply disappear if they are ignored or go unrecognized; rather, they act as destructive forces, seeking to remove the obstacles that prevent their natural expression. To come into relationship with this daemonic force obviously leads us outside the parameters of a religious way of life, as it is usually conceived.

My dream suggested to me the possibility of a middle way between repression and abandonment to the instincts through the cultivation of the anima function—as indicated by the female lion-handler. In practical terms, I discovered, this entailed shifting the locus of self-control from the head to the heart in order to engage with the instincts through feeling. From the marriage, or creative fusion, of differentiated feeling—the pure and authentic voice of the child—and the instinctual power drive and passion symbolized by the lion, a new fullness can be attained, a greater more integrated state of being can emerge: the Self. The feeding of the fish to the lion, and its reference to Christ, I understood as the need to direct the power of the instincts in service of the Self. This could only happen by enduring a veritable crucifixion of the "lower" animal nature—a theme that finds expression in the following painting.

Painting 23. Fiery Crucified Purple Serpent

A purple snake is mounted upon a luminous crucifix-shaped tree encircled by fire.

The purple snake might be taken as a symbol of Mercurius, who, in being subject to a crucifixion, reveals a symbolic identity with Christ.[30] In the drama of the Garden of Eden, we are accustomed to seeing the serpent as the evildoer, the one who corrupts and leads human beings to the Fall, into a world of separation from God, suffering, misery, and exile. But in the Gnostic vision, which fed into alchemy, we encounter a startling reversal. The role of the serpent is that of liberator, and it is Yahweh, the Creator, who is seen by the Gnostics as evil. Yahweh is the Demiurge, the creator of the false material world, who, aided by the Archons, keeps human beings in ignorance and entrapment, exiled from the unknown True God existing outside of Creation. In leading human beings to an awareness of the opposites through eating from the Tree of the Knowledge of Good and

Figure 21. Serpent Mercurialis Coiled around a Cross

Figure 22. The Mercurial Serpent Crucified

Evil, the serpent thus begins the process by which we, through inner gnosis, might find liberation by coming to an awareness of our divine essence and our relationship to the True God.

ENDNOTES

[1] Albert Einstein to Max Born, March 3, 1947, in *The Born-Einstein Letters: Friendship, Politics and Physics in Uncertain Times* (Basingstoke, UK: Macmillan Press, 2005), 155.

[2] Jacques Lyotard, *The Postmodern Condition: A Report on Knowledge*, translated by Geoff Bennington and Brian Massumi (Minneapolis, MN: Minnesota University Press, 1984), xxiii–xxiv.

[3] Jung, *Alchemical Studies*, par. 86, 59–60.

[4] Jung, *Psychology and Alchemy*, par. 29, 25.

[5] Jung, *Mysterium Coniunctionis*, par. 113, 94–95.

[6] Jung, *Mysterium Coniunctionis*, par. 658, 461.

[7] Jung, *Mysterium Coniunctionis*, pars. 10–12, 13–16, & par. 285, 216.

[8] Jung, *Mysterium Coniunctionis*, par. 252, 196.

[9] Carl Gustav Jung, *Aion: Researches into the Phenomenology of the* Self, second edition, volume 9, part II, of *The Collected Works of C. G. Jung*, translated by R. F. C. Hull (Princeton: Princeton University Press, 1969), par. 367, 232.

[10] Jung, *Mysterium Coniunctionis*, par. 127, 97 & par. 298, 225.

[11] Jung, *Mysterium Coniunctionis*, par. 660, 462.

[12] Jung, *Mysterium Coniunctionis*, par. 262, 204.

[13] Jung, *Mysterium Coniunctionis*, par. 140, 117.

[14] Jung, *Mysterium Coniunctionis*, par. 92, 112 (quoting Geber).

[15] Jung, *Mysterium Coniunctionis*, par. 113, 94.

[16] Jung, *Mysterium Coniunctionis*, par. 138, 114 (quoting from the *Rosarium Philosophorum*).

[17] Jung, *Mysterium Coniunctionis*, par. 151, 128.

[18] Jung, *Mysterium Coniunctionis*, par. 139, 115.

[19] See Jung, *Mysterium Coniunctionis*, par. 6, 7–8, & pars. 308–310, 230–231.

[20] Jung, *Mysterium Coniunctionis*, par. 172, 144–145.

[21] Jung, *Mysterium Coniunctionis*, par. 169, 142.

[22] Similar reptilian imagery is found in a number of Jung's paintings in *The Red Book*. See, for example, the images on pages 61, 119, and 129.

[23] Edinger, *Anatomy of the Psyche*, 12.

[24] The symbolic significance of the wolf and lion is explored by Edward Edinger in *Anatomy of the Psyche*, 18–20.

[25] Jung, *Mysterium Coniunctionis*, par. 405, 297.

[26] Jung, *Mysterium Coniunctionis*, par. 404, 295.

[27] Nietzsche, *Thus Spoke Zarathustra*, 54–56.

[28] Ross, *Gospel of Thomas,* 13.

[29] The Gospel of Thomas, Logion 70, from the Nag Hammadi Library, cited in Elaine Pagels, *The Gnostic Gospels* (New York: Vintage Books, 1979), xv.

[30] Cf. Jung, *Alchemical Studies*, par. 448, 333.

CHAPTER VIII
The *Cauda Pavonis*

The sequence of theriomorphic transformations of Mercurius eventually culminates with the appearance of the peacock's tail (the *cauda pavonis*) heralding the end of the *nigredo* and the new dawn that accompanies the brightness of the subsequent *albedo* phase. The peacock renews its plumage annually and is thus taken to be a symbol of rebirth and renewal, with its many-colored feathers, according to Jung, signaling the impending coalescence of the multiplicity of the elements or the psychological components into a unified whole represented by the philosopher's stone.[1]

Figure 23. The Peacock Rising from the Retort

Figure 24. The *Cauda Pavonis*

My own encounter with the peacock symbol came first in the form of a three-part synchronicity that encapsulated the main stages of the transformation process and anticipated the prospect of a future rebirth as the process unfolded. The synchronistic series occurred while I was on vacation on the Greek island of Rhodes in the summer of 2003. At that time, I was deep in emotional turmoil and struggling desperately with disturbing physical symptoms. The most alarming of these was the experience of choking and the sensation of being strangled. There was no obvious physical cause, I hasten to add, but I felt pressure around my neck, as if there were an assailant in the room strangling me. By now, I had grown accustomed to bizarre symptoms, but this one was particularly distressing. If ever I needed something to cast light on the meaning of my interminable suffering, to restore my shaken faith, and give me some greater symbolic perspective, it was now.

Such extreme conditions, when the ego is approaching the end of its tether and all seems lost, often call forth synchronicities by way of compensation or balance. Put in Jungian terms, synchronicities often occur when there is a "lowering of the threshold of consciousness."[2] Emotional affect is heightened and the unconscious grows in power relative to consciousness, which is in the dark, so to speak, for in such experiences one simply does not have access to the deeper meaning and pattern informing one's life. One is unconscious of this meaning, ignorant as to what is happening, and isolated in one's suffering and confusion. These conditions were very prevalent during that particular period of my life, reaching a climax during the vacation in Rhodes.

One afternoon, walking in the hills close to where we were staying, I came across the skeleton of a mountain goat in a derelict house. There was nothing especially unusual about this perhaps, although it had not happened to me before, but the sighting of the goat skeleton felt significant to me for the theme and experience of death were prominent in my life. Returning from my walk, I remarked on the discovery to Kathryn, but I did not stop to dwell on this again, and it passed from my mind.

A couple of days later, walking with Kathryn along the seafront road towards a restaurant in a neighboring town, I happened to glance down and was surprised to discover a snakeskin, perfectly intact, lying at my feet. Again, this struck me as unusual and it felt meaningful, but I did not give it much further attention as we continued on our way.

The next afternoon, however, as I lay on my bed in the hotel apartment, struggling through the strangulation experience, Kathryn called to me, in a mixture of bewilderment and excitement, from the balcony outside our room. As if from nowhere, a peacock had suddenly appeared and jumped up from the ground floor to our second-story apartment balcony and was now standing in close proximity to us (see figures 25 and 26). We were astonished. The atmosphere was incredibly thick and potent, charged with numinosity. The sighting felt not only highly improbable and inexplicable, but also in some sense miraculous. I should explain that peacocks were nowhere to be seen in the hotel grounds and we had not encountered them on the island itself. We did not see a peacock again during the remainder of our trip.

As we took in what we had experienced, I suddenly formed a connection between the three sightings, which became clearer to me as I reflected more in the days to follow. The goat skeleton I understood as a representation of the old ego structure that was dying. I knew of the goat as the symbol associated with the astrological zodiacal sign Capricorn, "ruled" by the planet Saturn, which is connected to the senex archetype, old age, structures, suffering, endings, time, and death. The snakeskin obviously suggested the process of rebirth, with the shedding of an old skin. I understood this symbol astrologically too, for the serpent is connected to the planetary archetype Pluto and its associated sign Scorpio, which in astrology is explicitly associated with transformation and rebirth. At that time, I had no idea what the peacock symbolized. But on returning home from the vacation I began to research its meaning. My studies of alchemy, over two years later, gave me the clearest insight into its significance as a central alchemical motif and herald of spiritual rebirth, marking the coming light of the *albedo* after the *nigredo*. I thus came to understand more fully the series of synchronicities as mapping out an entire cycle of the rebirth process: the death of the established ego-structure, the shedding of the old skin, and the birth into a new life and transformed psyche. This process has been a defining characteristic of my life experience for the last two decades.

Figure 25: Photograph of a Peacock on Apartment Balcony, Rhodes 2003

From that day forward, I have had multiple encounters with peacock symbolism, occurring in anticipation of, or in close coincidence with, numerous minor experiences of rebirth. Often, amidst the long struggle of transformation, I have the sense that my inner consciousness is being forced to pass through the containing structures of my old ego personality, emerging into a brighter, fuller reality on the other side—in the labor and birth experience that I described earlier. This birth transition is accompanied by a physical sensation of pressure on either side of my head, near the temples, and then a peculiar feeling of slowly easing or pushing through the constriction, like moving through a

Figure 26: Photograph of a Peacock and the Author, Rhodes 2003

tight passageway. The experience is often extremely uncomfortable, but ultimately impossible to stop. For it is as if my inner being has grown to the limits of the shell of my ego and has to break through, out of the shell (a theme depicted in Painting 24). Having passed through, I sometimes have the peculiar feeling that I am somehow taller, that I have stepped more fully into my being.

As I work through these transitions, peacock symbolism often enters my field of awareness one way or another. I might notice a peacock ornament while walking past a storefront or see peacocks in advertising materials or on greetings cards or very occasionally even come across real peacocks in the course of my day. Always, these encounters seem to herald an impending moment of rebirth, bringing a temporary end to a death process of the *nigredo*. Each mini birthing moment then instigates a new cycle, unfolding over many weeks or months.

151

Painting 24. Star and Broken Egg Shell

Painting 25. Rocket, Chaos, and Ravens

Painting 26. Rocket *Calcinatio*

Two other images related to the bright display of the *cauda pavonis* are the spectrum of colors of the rainbow and the dazzling explosions of a fireworks display. Both have similar symbolic connotations to the peacock. The suggestion, in the case of fireworks, is also the explosive release of energies accompanying rebirth and ecstatic liberation. In Grofian perinatal psychology, this imagery manifests towards the completion of the third stage of the birthing process (associated with the fetus's struggle through the birth canal), immediately before the birth experience itself. The rocket shapes in Painting 25 and Painting 26 convey just this kind of imagery.

ENDNOTES

¹ See Jung, *Mysterium Coniunctionis,* pars. 397–398, 290–291.

² See Jung, "Synchronicity," in *Structure and Dynamics of the Psyche*, par. 841, 36 & par. 856, 446.

CHAPTER IX
God, Sophia, and the Dark Spirit in Nature

During my crisis, as I struggled to come to terms with the split-off energies that held me in a state of agitation and distraction, manifesting in the strange bodily symptoms that left me feeling constantly alarmed, I wrestled inwardly with the question of the nature of God. I had first known and experienced a transcendent God of light and love in my under-graduate student years at Leeds, and I knew this loving power to be my origin and my destination. I knew, too, from other moments in my life of a personal God. I instinctively cultivated an inner dialogue with this God, who I thought of as my Father, in the deepest sense. I would experience this as a divine presence in times of need, and in rare moments I would be profoundly moved by this presence coming over me. These experiences were of a deity that was unquestionably good and loving. To be in the presence of God removed all suffering, rendered everything meaningful, and filled me with the radiant glow of wonder and mystery. But my crisis had introduced me to another type of presence and power. My dreams had named the figure as the Devil, but in general I just related to it as energy—trapped, split-off energy—compulsive and desperate in its emotional quality. For the most part, at that time the energy was manifesting as a cold sensation and loss of feeling in my lower leg or as blocks in my stomach.

One day, driven close to despair by my troubled state of mind and physical symptoms, I decided to try to dialogue with the energy, using something like the method of active imagination devised by Jung. I decided to talk to the energy as if it were a person and see if there might be any response. It was the first time I had ever attempted this kind of dialogue and I did not feel sure it would have value or deliver legitimate results. Nevertheless I proceeded, open to what might arise. I began by trying to let the energy speak. Almost immediately, the process gave voice to my (or its) experience of frustration at my wearying attempts to analyze and document my symptoms, struggles, and insights as I tried to find a way to resolve the crisis and heal myself.

Energy (E): I don't want to do work on myself any more. I'm so sick of it. I want to just get out there and live, take a few chances. I'm sick of just sitting around, doing nothing, waiting—sick of doing this stupid writing game, sick of you forcing me into things that are so dull it's killing me. No trick or technique is going to make me go away.

Me: Who are you?

E: I am the source of your life. I am the gushing overflow of love and passion for being alive.

Me: Why should I listen to you?

E: Do I need to answer that? Choose life and love or stagnation and death.

Me: Why do I have to abandon everything to follow you?

E: What is it you're giving up? Are these things so important to you?

Me: Some of them are, or they feel of value to me. I fear following you because you are not always present. When I try to follow you are gone and I freeze, and I am blocked by doubts. What if I follow you and you're gone? The life you promise seems so exciting and rich at the time. But there seems to be a certain underlying emptiness. Why do you have no concern for others' feelings, or for mine?

E: I am life bountiful and eternal, the wellspring of life. There is no death in me, so what is there to fear? I will be known to all people. I will lead them beyond themselves. I am joy and pain. I am the suffering of being alive. Not to feel pain is not to live. Things only seem empty when you think about them. I am not thought.

Me: Have you no concern or understanding for my predicament as a human being trying to live in the world?

E: You can become conscious of me.

Me: So I don't just hand over control to you?

E: You do that consciously.

Me: Do you have a name?

E: "ROAR OF THE OCEAN! SCREAM OF LIFE!" (I inwardly experience and hear the roar and a thunderous crack)

Me: You are so different from my personal relationship with God. Why is this?

E: Am I really so different?

Me: How can I communicate with you? How would you like to come through me?

E: I will guide your being if you will let me. Put aside conscious goals. Open yourself to me. Listen.

The dialogue seemed to me unquestionably authentic. I was not simply dreaming up words as answers, but was receiving answers from somewhere, something. The pronouncement of the name ("Roar of the ocean! Scream of life!") jolted me, for it took me totally by surprise. Inexplicably, I inwardly heard a kind of primeval roar of the power of nature and a thunderous crack, audible as an inner sensation. It was unlike any sound I had ever experienced.

Here, I later surmised, was a pagan deity, like Mercurius, Wotan, Pan, or Dionysus. The energy and qualities of these gods were now carried in the Christian myth by the figure of the Devil, but these qualities are not inherently evil. Rather, these figures symbolize the dark, because unconscious, power of nature. They are personifications of the dark spirit in nature, the unconscious god of nature. I gave visual form to this spirit, as the metamorphosizing corn spirit in Painting 17 and Painting 18.

Truly, this power seemed utterly incommensurable with the God I knew. But the enigmatic response ("am I really so different?") left open the possibility in my mind that the two powers—the God of light and love and the dark pagan instinctual spirit of nature—might ultimately be different expressions of one and the same all-encompassing divine ground. Were these two powers seeking to move together in and through my experience?

Reading *The Red Book* a decade after my crisis, I discovered that Jung had encountered a remarkably similar pagan god or nature power, described by the imaginal figure or "spirit guide" Elijah. His vision portrays the pagan primeval quality of the unknown God:

> The image that I saw was crimson, fiery colored, a gleaming gold. The voice that I heard was like distant thunder, like the wind roaring in the forest, like an earthquake. It was not the voice of my God, but it was a thunderous pagan roar, a call my ancestors knew but which I have never heard. It sounded prehistoric, as if from a forest on a distant coast; it rang with all the voices of the wilderness. It was full of horror yet harmonic.[1]

Jung gave dramatic expression, in the language of myth and religion, to this reawakening power, which in *The Red Book* is portrayed especially by the figure of Abraxas, named after a Gnostic deity. We see throughout Jung's own life a struggle to integrate his recognition of the dark power of the unconscious God into the classic Christian trinity. The dark spirit in nature can be conceived as an immanent and "feminine" form of the godhead, which the alchemical process seeks to unite with the transcendent "masculine" spirit.

Jung bemoaned Christianity's failure to deliver us collectively to anything approaching a realized psychological wholeness, for this cannot arise solely from subservience to a set of commandments and simply trying to be a good Christian, or even by imitating the ways of Jesus (the *imitatio Christi*). Christianity's ontological and ethical separation of good from evil, and the projection of evil onto the Devil, largely prevents an engagement with the instinctual drives (passions, fears, appetites) of the unconscious. For even to entertain these urges, and the fantasies that go with them, is to fall into sin, according to Christian dogma. Whereas Jesus Christ came to be portrayed as a figure of spotless purity, free from the stain of sin, Mercurius in alchemy is a figure as much instinctual and chthonic as spiritual. The alchemists, accordingly, more favorably disposed to the instincts and the spirit residing within the instincts, were able to move beyond Christianity in a genuine engagement with the darker side of life.

Everything we attribute to the figure variously named Lucifer, Satan, and the Devil, including the Dionysian energy of life, the passions, the instincts, the appetites, and those urges judged to be evil, are excluded from the Christian image of the divine and the character of Christ. This makes the Christ image very one-sided, Jung notes.[2] It does not reflect the wholeness of life, the totality of our psychological experience, but rather forces us to put ourselves in alignment with a narrow set of possible experiences and qualities, those deemed good in terms of Christian morality. Christian spirituality also excludes the material world, since the essence of Christ and God is transcendent, otherworldly. Jung makes the point that the Christian trinity—God the Father, Jesus the Son, and the

Holy Spirit—excludes the feminine too. Hence the great importance Jung placed on the Papal Decree of the Assumption of the Virgin Mary in 1950—a topic discussed in *Answer to Job*.[3] He believed this development represented a belated acknowledgment of the feminine as a fourth principle complementing the classical trinity, and an essential element of the godhead.

We can come to know the light half of the Self, symbolized by Christ, through a religious path of some sort. We might think, for example, of paintings depicting the love and purity of Christ or the transcendent bliss conveyed in sculptures of the Buddha. One can know the light side of the Self, perhaps through prayer and meditation, whatever one does with one's life, even if one does not engage with and live out one's passion. Hindu texts, such as the *Bhagavad Gita* and the *Upanishads*, also promote awareness of this eternal Self, within us, outside of time, outside of our human personality, and outside of the flux of events and the manifest world of phenomena. Attuning to this Self is presented as the aim of the spiritual life.

One only approaches the dark side of the Self, however, by coming to terms with one's daemon and the instinctual power of the unconscious. One comes to the dark Self through grappling with the instincts and one's passions. If the dark Self is not integrated, it can manifest (seemingly arbitrarily) as a tremendous destructive force or as some tragic plight that falls upon us. Jung realized that it is not enough just to live a religious life for one has to reckon with a power beyond the all-loving good side of God, a power that is amoral, when judged from the standpoint of conventional categories of good and evil. Job's confrontation with Yahweh in the Old Testament conveys this very point. The dialogues in *The Red Book* show Jung trying to come to terms with this dark spirit, imagined in the form of Abraxas. Like Abraxas, Mercurius in alchemy is a symbolic figure that portrays a more complete form of the Self, both light and dark, because it incorporates the realm of instinctual compulsion, which must be differentiated and transformed in the realization of the *lapis*.

The alchemists took Christianity as a starting point yet moved beyond its limitations in engaging with what they took to be the spiritual dimension of the material world. Following the alchemists, Jung served as a bridge to something beyond Christianity. He valued the Christian myth of the "inner man" and was concerned about the consequences if we were to lose this myth, and yet he was acutely aware of the problematic dimensions of a religious conception that set up sharp dichotomies between transcendent spirit and natural instinct. The dichotomy might well have been necessary in terms of collective psychological development during the Christian era, in that it furthered the development of individual consciousness by impelling us to choose against instinct, deny instinct, and thus develop our reasoning will and differentiating ego-conscious-ness. But now, I believe, we collectively face a challenge of a different order: we must come to terms with and integrate the instincts in the unconscious; to this end it is of little use to devalue the instincts as evil or to repress them.

As I have reflected on my experience in light of my studies of Jung and the wider field of the psychology of numinous experiences, I have come to the opinion that the recognition and the integration of the instinctual-spiritual power symbolized by the Abraxas-Dionysus-Wotan-Mercurius principle is the central spiritual and psychological task of our time. We live in a period of profound transition between the Christian era, confronted and mortally weakened by the rising might of science, and an as-yet-unknown emerging spiritual perspective or myth and an emerging new worldview. It is a challenge of planetary scope and significance to come to terms with the latent spiritual essence trapped in the darkness of human nature and the instinctual power of the animal-elemental sphere of life, especially when this power is scarcely recognized or named. To a large extent, it is a power known only through its varied problematic manifestations—in sickness and pathology, in devouring compulsions and obsessions, in barbarism and destructive acts of evil. Unrecognized, and antithetical to our moral values and ideals, the dark spirit tends to come to expression in a destructive form, as if it were seeking to remove the obstacles to its realization and integration into human consciousness.

The transcendent dimension of God, however, is not powerless and not a mere observer in this process, for its interventions offer direction and illuminating guidance as we struggle to face and integrate the dark power of the unconscious. The presence of the radiant star (in Painting 6 and Painting 16) suggests the role of the transcendent spiritual principle in my own experience. I am certain that I would not have been able to bear the intensity of the suffering I experienced had I not felt the reassuring presence and inspirational "pull" of the divine, which often manifested itself in moments of greatest need and seemed to me to be guiding the entire process. It became clear to me that this divine principle was supporting my struggle to overcome myself, and that it intended that I consciously engage and differentiate the instinctual sphere, and that I grow free of the incarcerating structures of the ego.

In the course of the alchemical process, Jung remarks, the transcendent principle is to be united with "the dark, chthonic aspect of nature"—the power described above—which, he explains, "is not *only* the darkness of the animal sphere, but rather a spiritual nature or a natural spirit."[4] This chthonic spirit, personified as Mercurius, is also the *anima mundi*, the world soul, that is thought to lie trapped within matter, caught up in the processes of nature, imprisoned in "'the chains' of Physis."[5] The transcendent principle is the "counsel of the spirit," which calls the soul to awaken from her slumber in matter and imposes upon the conscious ego the task of actualizing the soul's release.[6] I will explain shortly what this might mean in terms of personal experience.

We tend to imagine the nature of soul in Christian terms as the spiritual essence of our inner being. Soul, thus understood, is imagined as somehow housed within the body. It is an *individual* soul, belonging uniquely to us, inhering within us. In line with Platonic and Neoplatonic conceptions of an *anima mundi*, however, the alchemists also understood soul as a general principle that is inherent to all matter, entrapped in the material world, and in need of liberation. Our individual souls are embedded in a world soul.

The alchemists were influenced by Gnostic myths featuring Sophia, a deity personifying the feminine aspect of the divine, who (according to certain Gnostic accounts) acted unilaterally in bringing forth a son without the consent or involvement of the supreme spiritual Godhead. Because of this divine transgression, her son was imperfect and ignorant of the divine order, but had nevertheless inherited Sophia's immense creative power, with which he fashioned the world. He was named Yaldabaoth, the Demiurge, the creator of the world, but is an evil rather than benevolent power who, with the assistance of the Archons, keeps the soul, the spiritual essence buried within us, imprisoned in darkness and ignorance.[7] Filled with remorse, Sophia works with the Divine Father, the One True God, to effect the soul's release.

In other Gnostic accounts, Sophia herself becomes enamored with the realm of sense experience and undergoes a metaphysical fall into entrapment in the material world. The alchemists' spiritual mission was to help effect her release, reuniting Sophia, the immanent spiritual essence or soul in matter, with the transcendent divine. We might construe the transcendent divine here either as the Christian God the Father or, in Gnostic terms, as an unknown "alien" God outside of the world of space and time, beyond the Christian conception of God.[8] Either way, the alchemists were preoccupied with the work of the release of the "slumbering spirit" from the "'chains' of Physis" and the reunion of this recovered nature spirit with the transcendent godhead.

Informed by this Gnostic myth, then, alchemy pertains to the idea that within matter, and within the depths of the human psyche, there is a hidden spirit. I have referred to this, following Jung, as the dark spirit in nature.[9] There is a spiritual essence within the depths of nature, within the unconscious depths of human nature, which is seeking to emerge into consciousness but is bound up with and intimately embedded within the sphere of the drives, passions, and compulsions. The alchemist is charged with the task of trying to facilitate this release, such that the soul is no longer dominated by instinct.

Metaphysical and mythic accounts of transformative experiences, of the kind I passed through, might seem like nothing more than a superfluous overlay to a phenomenon that could be adequately or even fully described only in psychological terms. But recourse to metaphysical explanation imbues the experience with meaning beyond the merely personal fact of psychological crisis and transformation. It is a meaning suggested by spontaneous fantasies occurring during the process and confirmed, in my case at least, by numerous spiritual revelations that illuminated the way through. Ultimately, perhaps it is a question of innate temperament as to whether one needs such metaphysical explanations and whether or not they are revealed to one's consciousness.

In alchemy, as we have seen, these different levels of meaning and imagined purposes are enacted and realized through the intense labor of working with the matter in the laboratory, with the matter serving as the medium for the transformative drama. The emancipation of the *anima mundi* from matter equates in psychological terms to the separation of the soul, as an inner principle and quality of authentic feeling and inner knowing, from the appetites and desires of the body through a process known as *separatio*[10] (sometimes also referred to as the similar operation *distractio*).[11] As the alchemist might cut apart or heat matter in the *vas alembic*, revealing moisture trapped within, so the soul—the "moisture" of differentiated feeling trapped within the unconscious instincts—might be accessed and released.

We can envisage an unconscious *separatio* as the experience of dismemberment when the psyche fragments and falls apart into its multiplicity. By contrast, we might imagine a conscious *separatio* as the act of discrimination of thoughts, feelings, and motivations from each other. During individuation, thoughts and motive impulses are no longer left to their own devices, but each emotion and accompanying idea is to be examined, differentiated, and distinguished from the conscious ego. That is, we learn to distinguish the sense of "I" from the morass of fantasies, emotions, and thoughts that move through our awareness. In a sustained act of conscious interrogation of the psyche, as we begin to recognize and catch the way we are "possessed" by particular urges and fantasies, we no longer function instinctively and unconsciously. The natural state of unconscious wholeness is increasingly eroded in the act of identifying and distinguishing the various sets of archetypal fantasies at play in the psyche.

The *separatio* functions like a slashing blade, allowing us to dissect emotional affects as they come over us. This enables us, in time, to distinguish what the emotion or drive would have us think and do from our true feelings. It permits the differentiation of the anima, as Jung has described this process elsewhere. By engaging with our fantasies, desires, and emotional reactions, it becomes possible to distinguish the voice of the soul, the "still small voice" within. As we learn to recognize it, this voice or inner feeling emerges as a psychological function alongside thinking and reason. In making decisions, we can call upon this function to help us feel into the "rightness" of things. Often the anima can guide us where reason fails, for the anima possesses a mysterious connection to the transrational order behind our lives. This order is in turn symbolized by the archetype of the spirit, often in the form of the mythic figure of the wise old man. In this way, the anima offers a mode of connection to the Self.

A visionary experience in 2004 introduced me to the anima, as a personified figure, emerging into my conscious awareness. One day, alone in my room, I was feeling pursued as always by inner fears and the automatic reaction of pushing them away. But on this occasion, for some reason I found that I was able to allow myself to turn to face the fears. My anxious defensiveness against the fears spontaneously subsided and I was rewarded with a moving experience of a deep emotional core revealing itself from within the darkness of what I took to be my shadow. My reflections in my journal entry from 2004 relay the essence of this encounter:

> The shadow wanted recognition and my friendship, which I gave. It was a universal power, but so lonely, as its approach causes such fear that people constantly run from it and in its presence are driven by fear to evil. But behind this darkness, the shadow brings "moisture" to our lives, a deep context and contour. It is old, ancient, deep—as deep as can be. It is dense and animating—a great but sad being who returned my friendship and could help me out, and give to me that which I don't have.

In turning towards my fears, and entering into communion with the shadow, I had the experience of the enveloping darkness parting or dissipating to reveal an inner figure of dark feminine beauty, of a blue-purple hue, coming forward within me. In facing my fears, the shadow, I later concluded, had revealed the archetypal form of the anima, the soulful feminine essence that could lend richness and deep feeling to my experience, bringing emotional discernment and texture.

This visionary experience of the anima was soon to be followed by another vivid imaginal encounter—this time with the Self.

ENDNOTES

[1] Jung, *Red Book,* "Scrutinies," 357.

[2] See Jung, *Psychology and Alchemy,* pars. 1–42, 147.

[3] See Carl Gustav Jung, *Answer to Job. The Problem of Evil: Its Psychological and Religious Origins,* translated by R. F. C. Hull (Cleveland, OH, and New York: Meridian Books, 1970), 182, 187–198.

[4] Jung, *Mysterium Coniunctionis,* par. 427, 310.

[5] Jung, *Mysterium Coniunctionis,* par. 673, 472.

[6] Jung, *Mysterium Coniunctionis,* par. 673, 472.

[7] See Willis Barnstone and Marvin Meyer, *The Gnostic Bible,* revised and expanded edition (Boston, MA: Shambhala Publications, 2009), 166–185.

[8] For an account of the "alien" God in Gnosticism, see Hans Jonas, *The Gnostic Religion: The Message of the Alien God and the Beginnings of Christianity,* third edition (Boston, MA: Beacon Press, 2001).

[9] See, for example, Jung, *Mysterium Coniunctionis,* par. 427, 310.

[10] See Jung, *Mysterium Coniunctionis,* par. 696, 488–489.

[11] The *distractio,* Jung informs us, is the process which brings about the end of the state in which "the affectivity of the body has a disturbing influence on the rationality of the mind" (Jung, *Mysterium Coniunctionis,* par. 671, 471).

CHAPTER X
Coniunctio in California

In August 2004, after more than two years of being incapacitated by psychological and physical pathology and in the grip of a titanic inner struggle, I succeeded in moving from Wales to San Francisco to begin graduate school at CIIS. Kathryn remained behind in Wales initially, with the plan that she would join me at a later point once I had determined if things would work out and I had established a base.

I am well aware, looking back now, that from the outside this move might have seemed like a radical and ill-advised attempt at a solution to my predicament. I knew well enough that in moving 5000 miles to another country on my own I risked heaping stress and trauma onto my original trauma—indeed, I had already suffered something of this kind less than a year before, in September 2003, when I had travelled to the U.S. alone in the hope of breaking free of my crisis. That particular trip proved catastrophic. In a desperate, panic-stricken state of mind, restlessly wandering from place to place in California, I barely survived with my sanity intact and came close to losing touch with reality. I returned home defeated. It took me months to recover.

By the summer of 2004, however, I became persuaded by my growing inner conviction and encouraging synchronicities that enrolling at CIIS was the right course of action. And so it proved, for attending CIIS brought me into an environment in which I could study subjects related to just the kind of transformative crisis I was passing through, which significantly aided my recovery. Above all, it was the move I needed to make to satisfy the powerful energies within me, and to direct my instincts and emotions towards a spiritual end.

By my thirty-second birthday, in November 2004, I felt that I had begun to return to myself. The long inner struggle to master the fears and compulsive drives within me was the bedrock of my recovery. Moving to San Francisco to pursue my passion had enabled me to pass beyond the *nigredo*-dominated phase of the process, bringing a sense, intermittently, of emergence into the brightness of the *albedo*, and allowing me to reconnect to the flow of life moving through me. I had been able to redirect my energies from the underworld struggle back towards an extraverted engagement with the world—the *rubedo* phase.

The process of rebirth, I have found, continues to cycle between *nigredo*, *albedo*, and *rubedo* experiences—even today, almost twenty years later. Mini death and rebirth experiences have become for me a way of life, with each successive death often seeming more complete, more final, more absolute, as if I am dying little by little to my old self, being broken down, submitting to my wholeness, relinquishing control to the power that had revealed itself to me in my active imagination in 2003. In this sense, with the cyclical movement of one phase to another, there is not strictly speaking a process of linear development. But, in terms of a chronological trajectory, I look back on the period of 2001 to late 2004 as dominated by the *nigredo*, in that themes and experiences of entrapment, suffering, death, dismemberment, inner conflict, and chaos were almost always prominent. This period was the critical phase in my crisis of transformation.

As the *nigredo* themes moved more into the background of my life in late 2004, the primary challenge for me thereafter was remaining in watchful control of my passion. I was living in a city that I loved, studying the subjects that I loved. I had invested a lot in the enterprise and taken enormous risks with my life that had impacted those I was close to, especially my wife. In terms of vocation, I knew I could not really do anything else with my life. I felt I had little choice in the matter. I therefore felt powerfully stirred to make my mark and to follow this path to its logical conclusion. The intensity of my drive to succeed and the evocative nature of the material I was studying often gripped me so powerfully that I could barely handle the emotional force within me. Because I had not been able to give expression to my feelings in the act of living for such a long time, my emotional nature remained extremely charged. I had to maintain a hyper-vigilant awareness of my inner process. I lived in close proximity to the unconscious, still often at the mercy of activated drives and fantasies. While in the classroom for lectures, I sometimes felt as if I were holding back a tidal wave of emotion or drive while performing a kind of psychological open-heart surgery—for, out of necessity, I was carefully monitoring and dissecting the motivations behind the drives that were exerting a pull over me. I would watch diligently when and how I would get caught by a particular emotion or thought and react compulsively to it. With each instance of conscious recognition of being caught, possessed by a particular impulse, I would then repeatedly return my attention to my heart and pit my will and intention against the impulse as it pulled at me and grabbed me. It was through this method, applied over many months and years, that I was able to overcome the worst effects of the compulsive power of the unconscious and escape domination by it.

I recall at that time, having passed through the major period of my crisis, that I sometimes felt bullet-proof. I felt in one sense that I had already died and thus no harm could come to me. Any life experiences from this point on were a bonus. In grappling with underworld energies, and in recovering them consciously, I felt buoyed by a flow of power that propelled me forward in life with an intense singular purpose and will to succeed. In the flow of this power, I also began to feel more unified.

The process of unification continued throughout that year. Towards the end of 2004, with Kathryn having joined me in San Francisco for a month-long visit, I began to have dreams featuring the juxtaposition of pairs of opposites, such as sweet and sour or black and white foods, and old and young or male and female animals, as the opposites within me were becoming progressively more integrated. I felt that the acutely painful inner division that had blighted my life had now been bridged in some significant way. The following dream appeared to confirm this feeling, first revisiting some of the earlier *sublimatio* themes but then concluding with marriage as a symbol of the conjunction of opposites.

I am outside a cathedral like Notre-Dame (or perhaps Grace Cathedral in San Francisco). It is the day of my wedding [in reality Kathryn and I were married in 2000] *and many guests are gathered outside waiting for the ceremony. A large builder's crane is there and I climb up onto the arm of the crane. As it moves, swinging through the air, I struggle to maintain my grip. I am dizzy from the height, barely able to hang on. I look at the cathedral and see on the outer wall a sequence of three images depicted, perhaps in stained glass or in stone, that represent the process I had been through. The last image is still to be completed and this shows a child standing beside a round stone. The crane arm swings and lowers me into the cathedral. Inside, I am with my bride (my wife) and I partake in the wedding ceremony. My aunt (a spiritualist and medium) is there. A voice says: "Now you are married!"*

Figure 27. *Sponsa* and *Sponsus, Coniunctio* Image

Again, the religious setting of the dream made clear to me its spiritual significance, with Notre-Dame indicating a connection to my earlier Paris dream in the hotel room and also to the dream set on Church Street in my hometown. Kathryn and I had also taken our honeymoon in Paris in 2000.

From the dizzying heights of my *sublimatio* ascent, in this dream I now found myself enacting something like a sacred marriage through the wedding ceremony, with my aunt as a witness and spiritual midwife. The incomplete third image, that of a child and a stone, implied, I believe, that the transformative sequence of the conjunction would continue to unfold. The coming together of "masculine" ego-consciousness and the "feminine" instinctual unconscious in an alchemical marriage is the prelude to the birth of the child and stone—both symbols of the Self, in Jung's view.[1]

Alchemical work and the process of individuation seek to effect the *coniunctio* of the conscious ego with its unconscious ground, personified as the union of *Sol* and *Luna* or *Rex* and *Regina*. It could be said that the

Painting 27. Child, Gold, Bird, Serpent

173

transformative process begins and ends with the *coniunctio*. It is initiated by a coming together of consciousness with the unconscious, as the ego faces the shadow in the *nigredo*—this is a so-called lesser *coniunctio*. The opposites are then further pulled apart, in a painful process of separation, as the ego comes to distinguish itself from the archetypal fantasies and drives of the unconscious. The separation and work of differentiation then make possible a movement towards a subsequent reunion of conscious-ness with the unconscious, described by Edinger as a greater *coniunctio*.[2] It was with this process in mind that Jung, writing *Mysterium Coniunctionis*, chose as the explanatory subtitle "an inquiry into the separation and synthesis of psychic opposites."

The Self as the new center of the psyche is the product of the "chymical marriage," of *Rex* and *Regina* or *Sol* and *Luna*.[3] While the Self is present all along (it is, as Jung explains, "an *a priori* existent out of which the ego evolves"), it is also effectively "born" within us, as it emerges into conscious awareness.[4] In terms of the progression of the encounter with archetypes during individuation, the Self is to be realized through an encounter with the anima-animus principles. As Jung remarked, the Self is the "child" of the pregnant anima.[5]

Like many people with some knowledge of Jungian psychology, I would imagine, before entering my crisis I had a vague sense of the Self as psychological wholeness. I had an intuition of what wholeness might be like, and my spiritual experiences had given me firsthand knowledge of a superordinate power dwarfing my personal will and ego. But in late 2004 and into 2005 I came to a more concrete sense of the Self, heralded principally by a visionary experience.

One afternoon, I was working alone in the bookstore at CIIS—a position I had held since late August 2004, just after I arrived in San Francisco. The store was quiet, and my attention was focused, as usual, on my inner process. By now, I was accustomed to maintaining an acute vigilance of my psyche but, in spite of my best efforts, I could not prevent myself on occasion falling under the consuming influence of the drives and fantasies moving through me. On that day, however, the struggle reached a point of decisive transition, precipitated by the experience of surrender. I recorded the experience in a journal at the time:

> As I gave in today at the bookstore, just sitting, resigned, realizing everything I did was futile, I sensed the feeling of stone, an eternal changeless stone. This was a presence subtly permeating my consciousness. Then I felt and inwardly saw a mountain emerging within me, like a giant whale surfacing from the water. And this stone, this mountain/whale, I could worship, and it was me, it was the Self which, when I ceased, was there, in the midst of things, eternal and steadfast.

The image revealed to me something imperishable and immutable, something immense and eternal, standing in contrast to the volatility of my emotional state. The fiery waves of my instincts could wash over me, but now, from here on, they would hit against the immovable inner mountain that had become established as a new center of my being. From that moment, although my struggle did not cease, I felt significantly more solid and anchored, as if I now had the security of an inner core, like the stone of the alchemical philosophers. My center had emerged and was to remain.

I did not feel that the transformative process was over—far from it. But I sensed that something had changed within me. A threshold had been crossed. The image of the whale-mountain seemed like the culmination of a long struggle for a center, which could compensate for the volatility of my emotional state. It was a decisive development in the establishment of a new psychological structure.

ENDNOTES

[1] The motifs of the child and the stone were both central to the inner meaning of Jung's own life. In an inscription on a stone monument in his tower at Bollingen, he had chiseled in Greek the following words: "Time is a child—playing like a child—playing a board game—the kingdom of the child. This is Telesphoros, who roams through the dark regions of this cosmos and glows like a star out of the depths. He points the way to the gates of the sun and to the land of dreams" (Jung, *Memories, Dreams, Reflections,* 254).

[2] For explanations of the lesser *coniunctio* and greater *coniunctio*, see Edinger, *Anatomy of the Psyche,* 211.

[3] Jung, *Mysterium Coniunctionis,* par. 104, 89.

[4] Carl Gustav Jung, "Transformation Symbolism in the Mass" (1954) in *Psychology and Religion: West and East,* volume 11 of *The Collected Works of C. G. Jung,* translated by R. F. C. Hull (Princeton: Princeton University Press, 1969), par. 391, 259.

[5] See Jung, *Mysterium Coniunctionis,* par. 217, 176.

CHAPTER XI

The *Unio Mystica* and the Transformation of the World

The three-phase image of transformation in my Notre-Dame/Grace Cathedral dream, all the details of which, regrettably, I could not fully remember on awaking, parallels the three-phase model of the alchemical conjunction put forward in the work of sixteenth-century Belgian alchemist Gerhard Dorn, which Jung discusses in detail in *Mysterium Coniunctionis*. His analysis of Dorn's theory, it might be said, is the climax and culmination of his studies of alchemy, perhaps also of his entire life's work, providing a framework within which to understand the transformative opus in its entirety, in terms of both its microcosmic and macrocosmic significance. The phases might be summarized as follows:

1. The *unio mentalis*, or mental union.
2. The reunion of the *unio mentalis* with the body.
3. The *unio mystica* or *mysterium coniunctionis*.

Although the three phases are all placed within the conjunction, implying a coming together and union, it should be noted that the process also entails separation and differentiation, as part of the larger union and synthesis.

From the initial state of unconscious wholeness, out of the dark unity of the *unio naturalis*, consciousness gradually develops around an emerging ego and sense of autonomous individual identity, with the individual increasingly relying on the capacity to exercise reason and will. The long course of human psychological evolution has delivered us to this point, especially with the accelerated change of the modern era and the concomitant rise of the rational ego. Today, the still-developing ego, carrier of self-reflective consciousness, exists in a state of fluctuating antagonism and compromise with our instinctual nature, yet the overall unity of the psyche remains largely intact.

For a minority of people, however, at a certain point of psychological development this original unity might be lost entirely. Then, as Jung notes in his discussion of Nietzsche, the "One becomes Two"—the two systems of the psyche are torn apart.[1] This break can be traumatic ("a moment of deadliest peril!"), as I experienced firsthand, and it can lead one towards disturbing states, even to psychosis and schizophrenia.[2] But the rupture permits and is caused by the emergence of the Self, and in this sense it is a progressive, if perilous and uncertain, phase of transition. Through the resulting schism in the structure of the psyche the Self emerges from the dark depths, where it might become established as the new psychological and existential center.

Looking back, I realized that acting in accord with my loosely rational plan for life, prioritizing this plan over my feelings and the energies of the body, had forced upon me a dramatic severance of the two psychological systems—rational consciousness and the instinctual-emotional power of the unconscious. Although I initially experienced this split as pathological and therefore wholly undesirable, the result of a dangerously one-sided denial of my emotions, I later came to see that it forced me into just this kind of accelerated mode of psychological transformation. Individuation involves a tearing free of consciousness from its containment in the world of instinct. In ideal circumstances, the separation could unfold progressively, in relatively stable psychological conditions, rather than as the traumatic crisis I had experienced. But, because of the sudden irreversible severance, I was compelled, if I wished to survive and live any kind of fulfilling life, to try to bring the two systems back together in a new synthesis. I had no choice in the matter. To this end, as I sought to make sense of what I'd been through, the alchemical descriptions of the "separation and the synthesis of psychic opposites" through the stages of the conjunction were to be extremely instructive.

As the first phase of the conjunction, the *unio mentalis* represents a critical element of this process. It might be described, following Jung's interpretation of Dorn, as the union of ego-consciousness and its rational-spiritual perspective with the "spirit" or "soul" liberated, figuratively speaking, from the unconscious world of matter and the body. In the language of the alchemists, the natural state of *unio naturalis*, in which the soul is inextricably bound up with the bodily sphere, is brought to an end by freeing the soul from the body. The alchemist then seeks to effect a union of conscious reason ("spirit") with the liberated soul, bringing to completion the arduous first stage of the *coniunctio*.

More technically, the *unio mentalis* is created by the coming together of ego-consciousness with some psychological essence that has been liberated from the unconscious. As Jung puts it: "the coniunctio appears here as the union of a consciousness (spirit), differentiated by self-knowledge, with a spirit abstracted from previously unconscious contents."[3] Effectively, its realization is close in meaning to what Jung understands as individuation. It constitutes both a progressive tearing free of consciousness from the unconscious realm of instinct and then a union of this new consciousness ("spirit") with the ego, incrementally expanding the scope of consciousness.

Every act of intentional consciousness, directed by reason and in accordance with an ascribed morality, against our unconscious instinctive responses to life, against the flow of feeling and habitual inclination, breaks the hold of unconscious nature over us, and marks a step towards the realization of the *unio mentalis*. Thus Jung praises the British "stiff upper lip," as a great psychological achievement, with its posture of refusal to be dominated by the pull of the emotions or even to show emotions, although this posture is as likely to result in repression as genuine psychological transformation, it has to be said. The same is true of Christianity, the most significant moral influence on the West. Each instance of adhering to religious doctrine and moral prescriptions, in defiance of instinctive responses to life, helps to remove us from the state of unconscious wholeness, as we gradually transition to a life directed by intentional consciousness rather than instinctual patterns. In trying to live morally, we refuse to succumb to lust and rage, for instance, thereby strengthening reasoning consciousness against the drives of the unconscious.

But the *unio mentalis* is far more than just the denial of the emotions and instincts, by pitting reason against them. For that denial, in establishing the autonomy of the ego, only holds the instincts and emotions at bay, often by repressing them into the unconscious. Rather, to achieve the *unio mentalis* one must experience, contain, and probe the emotions, drives, and fantasies as they arise. Then, through persistence, steadfastness, understanding, and insight, one can break the binding power of the instincts and liberate the consciousness or feeling contained within them.

In Jung's view, the collective unconscious contains sparks of "spirit" or consciousness buried within the darkness of the instinctual sphere.[4] One can imagine these sparks as stars in the enveloping darkness of the night sky or as specks of gold trapped in the dark depths of the ocean floor. The operations performed on Mercurius, trapped in the vessel, enable these sparks of "spirit" to be released and gathered. My own paintings convey something of this kind. In Painting 5, for instance, specks of gold appear within the darkness of the pool.

Put differently, we might say that we must contain and control our instincts, desires, impulses, and so forth, and then differentiate or dissect them through an act of conscious discrimination—recall our earlier discussion of *separatio*. We allow ourselves to experience what the desire or fantasy wants of us, but we must hold that desire in tension with our conscious rational-spiritual position. For example, one might aspire towards universal compassion and the dedication of one's life to a noble cause only to find that one's desires compulsively pull one in other directions—towards crude excitement or sensual gratification, perhaps, or to a fearful self-protectiveness and defensiveness or to power-driven ambition. If one has a clear sense of one's highest ideals, perhaps derived from moments of spiritual realization or from an inner voice of calling and conscience, one can cleave to these ideals and use one's commitment to them against the pull of the "lower" instincts. One can become aware of how one is unconsciously "grabbed" by impulses not in accord with one's spirituality and consciously chosen commitment to one's higher possibilities. With good will and persistence, one can train oneself to experience but resist and overcome the pull of these compulsive impulses, and then to reconcile them with consciousness. In Jungian psychology the reconciliation takes place through the emergence of a new symbol, serving the psyche's transcendent function, as Jung named it. This is the dialectical procedure at the heart of alchemy. The ultimate aim of this procedure is that we might benefit from the motive power of instinct but not be compulsively driven and controlled by it. Thus one might still act on one's power drive and passion, for these energies are the motive forces of life. But one does so less compulsively, with the drives now sublimated in service of the Self or integrated aspects of the wholeness of the Self.

I have described earlier how I employed something like this technique to find a way through my crisis. Under the influence of a powerful emotional reaction or urge, I would hold my attention firmly on my heart, or take control of my breath, and struggle against the impulses arising within me that would automatically seize my attention, pulling it elsewhere, or stir me to restless action in a pattern of deeply ingrained, automatic avoidance. Through this ascetic discipline I was able to access the underlying motivations within the urges that were coming over me. Often, my desiring and anxious restlessness, I came to see, grew out of a deep-seated self-protective response to life and a conditioned unwilling-ness to face the fullness of experience in the moment, especially emotional pain or shame. The "careful investigation of desires and their motives," as Jung described the essential task of the first stage of the conjunction, enabled me to begin to break the binding power of the unconscious that had kept me imprisoned for so long.[5] The whale-mountain experience marked a culmination of this process. Looking back, with an alchemical framework in mind, I came to see this as a significant step in the larger ongoing process of the realization of the *unio mentalis*.

The *unio mentalis*, Jung remarks, results in the attainment of self-knowledge and produces "a realistic and more or less non-illusory view of the outside world."[6] One can see the world as it really is only when one is not unconsciously reacting to urges and impulses and fantasies that pull one away from the conscious experience of the moment. Until then, one exists in the Maya-like delusory world of fantasies, caught in incessant projecting onto the world and restless desiring, dominated by the unconscious id, to put this in Freudian terms. By a withdrawal of projections and ascetic self-denial, it is possible, Jung explains, to bring an end to the ego's "unconscious identity with the object"[7] and grow free of "the turbulence of the emotions"[8] such that the soul no longer "desires 'beyond physical necessity.'"[9]

The attainment of the *unio mentalis* marks a significant, and, by all accounts, rarely achieved stage in the overcoming of the compulsive and binding element of our instinctual-desire nature. The result of this process is the delivery to a state of inner surety that arises from having faced and overcome the devouring power of the unconscious. The person who has successfully passed through this process, Jung notes, perhaps in reference to his own experience,

> . . . has a genuine claim to self-confidence, for he has faced the dark ground of his self and thereby has gained himself. This experience gives him faith and trust, the *pistis* in the ability of the self to sustain him, for everything that menaced him from the inside he has made his own. He has acquired the right to believe that he will be able to overcome all future threats by the same means. He has arrived at an inner certainty which makes him capable of self-reliance, and attained what the alchemists called the *unio mentalis*.[10]

I too, after the prolonged period of suffering, arrived at a place of hard-earned confidence from having overcome that which had afflicted me, at least to the extent that I could resume my life. The inner certainty, in my case, was symbolized in the vision of the whale/mountain, just as for the alchemists the solidity and imperturbable quality was embodied by the *lapis* and the incorruptible nature of gold. I felt that I had won through to some degree of self-mastery that enabled me to move forward in life, confident that I could face any further adversities the psyche might bring my way. This did not signal triumphant resolution, for experiences of rebirth to this day remain a frequent occurrence in my life. However, by that time, in fall 2004, I knew was able to face and be alone with my psyche, whatever states of mind and emotions arose. It was this emerging confidence that enabled me to make the move to California, culminating in the whale experience.

Needless to say, the emergence of this inner certainty is not the endpoint. Two further stages remain in the larger process of the conjunction. The second stage, according to Dorn, is the *reunion* of the separated *unio mentalis* with the body, bringing about a "reanimation" of the body.[11]

As Dorn envisages it, the withdrawal of the soul from the body during the *unio mentalis* leaves the body and the world "dead," because the soul is the animating principle of the body and of life in general.[12] Thus Jung describes the anima, associated with the soul, as the archetype of life, carrying forth and personifying Eros as the fundamental life urge, that which makes us feel alive, in touch with the wellsprings of life. In the conjunction, the body is not to be discarded in some kind of detached transcendent realization or dissolution of embodied selfhood. Alchemy, despite its asceticism, affirms the body; it is not held to be inherently corrupt or bad. Rather, the *unio mentalis* is intended to free the body from the corruption of the passions, which cause the soul to "desire 'beyond physical necessity.'"[13] The *separatio* liberates the soul from the domination by desire and frees one from instinctual compulsion. The sulphuric compulsion in desire is burnt out and purified.

The first phase of the *coniunctio*, then, brings about a kind of psychological severance of the consciousness from the animating power of the instincts. It leads us temporarily to a place of calm detachment and equanimity, untouched by the pulse of life, desire, and passion. Reengaging with the world, however, more or less immediately brings us back into relationship with the life urge and the flow of desiring. If we then consent to desire, give in to it and let ourselves go, we will feel whole again, as if our energies and drives have been fully restored. This can feel euphoric, but if we are not vigilant the reactivation of instinct can result in a *regressive* wholeness, bringing about a relapse to the former state of domination by instinct. All the gains in consciousness might be lost. Each time there is a reunion of the separated *unio mentalis* with the body there is a danger of falling under the sway of instinct—indeed, in practice this is perhaps unavoidable to some degree. Mercurius breaks loose again and has to be brought back under control. The controlling of activated instinct is the basis for the next step towards the *unio mentalis* in a repeating cycle.

"Had they brought about the reunion in a direct way," Jung notes, in reference to the alchemists' approach to the reunion,

> the soul would simply have snapped back into its former bondage and everything would have been as before. The volatile essence so carefully shut up and preserved in the Hermetic vessel of the *unio mentalis* could not be left to itself for a moment, because this elusive Mercurius would then escape and return to its former nature.

Given free rein, the soul would "slip back into its former unconsciousness without taking with it anything of the light of the spirit into the darkness of the body."[14]

We can imagine a situation in which the changing events of our lives constantly cause us to fall back on our instincts. Each situation we might face, in spite of our best efforts to remain conscious, centered, and poised, tends to stir compulsive affect and instinctual reactions, such that we relapse into old attitudes and ways of being, or become aware of how we have unconsciously identified with particular desires, feelings, ideas, and ways of seeing ourselves and the world. I believe this is what Jung means by the alchemists repeatedly discovering where their "attitude is still defective."[15] We fall, again and again from the purity of spiritual feeling and a state of quiet enchantment into the corruption of the instincts, perhaps driving us to try to desperately save ourselves, or to pursue excitement, power and influence, and sensual satisfaction. And we must fall in this way, for only in succumbing to the drives and passions of the instincts, only by entering into them, can they be transformed, and the compulsion within them overcome. Thus to live alchemically is to move back and forth between states in which instincts are stirred and periods of ascetic inward concentration by which we can break free of our identification with the instincts and move to a more spiritualized transformed condition.

In navigating the reunion with the body, the aim is to move through to a new, higher state of wholeness. There is a kind of creative fusion of consciousness with the dynamisms of the body that brings healing and renewal. Perhaps for this reason Jung contemplated "the fission and fusion of the psychic opposites" as an alternative subtitle for the English version of *Mysterium Coniunctionis*, at the suggestion of his translator, R. F. C. Hull.[16] This fusion is symbolically depicted in alchemy as the creation of a magical *caelum* or quintessence or healing balsam, "the admixture of honey, magic herbs, and human blood" that is a symbolic prefiguration of the self.[17] The *caelum* is akin to the mediating symbol that serves as a bridge between the opposites and psychic systems, healing the painful condition of inner division.[18] While the alchemists themselves may have aspired to create such a balsam or *caelum* in chemical form, through the mixture of various ingredients, in psychological terms we can imagine the *caelum* as forged from the various components of the psyche. On occasion, I have the sense that my own alchemical transition, as it continues to unfold, brings forth the different elements of my psyche in such a way that each "ingredient," each complex or subpersonality within me, contributes something essential to the wholeness of what I am. Even undesirable traits, such as anger and vengefulness and resentment, have their rightful place in the containing wholeness of the psyche, organized around the Self. In rare moments, the realization has come over me that one is led by the process to offer each part of oneself in a kind of sacred sacrifice on the altar of the Self—not just the spiritual or higher enlightened parts, but the instinctual and chthonic parts too. Moving back and forth among the various aspects of the psyche effectively draws together the scattered pieces of the Self, gathers up the sparks of consciousness or spirit previously buried within the darkness of the unconscious.

Moving beyond this state too, however, the alchemical opus aspires towards more than exclusively individual healing and transformation. The third phase of the conjunction is the *mysterium coniunctionis* or *unio mystica*, which is tantamount to a union of the individual with "the eternal Ground of all empirical being."[19] Here Dorn and Jung depart from each other, for this phase is mysticism, plain and simple. Jung does conceive of individuation as a "'mysterium coniunctionis'," with "the self being experienced as a nuptial union of opposite halves" but for the most part he rests content with construing this union in psychological terms.[20] Yet the essence of the practice of alchemy—the very fact that the alchemist was working to transform matter in the alembic and in the process transforming his or her own psyche—implies that the significance of the transformation might extend beyond the individual psyche to the world at large. After all, as we have already considered, the metaphysical aim of the alchemical opus was to free the soulful essence of Sophia from her entrapment in the material sphere. In the *unio mystica*, the third phase of the conjunction, this aim is to be realized as the soulful essence of the feminine slumbering spirit is unified with the transcendent spiritual ground of all things. The alchemist is made one with the spiritual source of existence.

Seen in this way, individuation is not only a model of psychological transformation of the individual person but a way of participation in the spiritual transformation of the entire universe. It has not only a microcosmic significance but a macrocosmic one. It is not only psychological in its essence but metaphysical, not only human but divine, concerned with the transformation of the godhead.

In attempting to comprehend in concrete terms the relationship of the three stages and how they fit together, reflecting on my own experience I came to see the *unio mentalis* and the reunion of the separated *unio mentalis* with the body as an ongoing back and forth that repeats cyclically as the transformative process unfolds during the course of individuation. First one breaks the hold of some state of compulsive emotion and instinct over one, then, from a position of temporary detached calm, one reengages with life and therefore with the instincts (the reunion phase). Each time there is a kind of mini death, and the psyche restructures itself (the *coagulatio*) in progressive steps towards wholeness. I see both these phases then as subsets of the third phase—that of the *mysterium coniunctionis*—rather than the third phase as something one moves to *after* individual transformation is complete. In overcoming oneself again and again, the more aligned one's individual being becomes with being at large. Logically, at some point, the mystical union must bring about a total reconciliation of one's individual being with the world, of consciousness with the unconscious, and of the individual with the divine—although obviously this might be an ideal than an actually attainable end. The *unio mystica* implies a state of unity in which one becomes a total match for the world such that there is no incongruence between one's own nature and any aspect of life. In this spiritualized state, the life force animating the world at large spontaneously acts through us, for our own inner nature has become one with the inner nature of the world and we are able to live in absolute harmony with the Tao-like flow of meaning and life energy moving through us. Through the completion of the *coniunctio* and the transformation of the individual, the world itself is transformed.

ENDNOTES

¹ Jung, "Concerning Rebirth" in *Archetypes and the Collective Unconscious*, par. 217, 121 (quoting Nietzsche).

² Jung, "Concerning Rebirth" in *Archetypes and the Collective Unconscious*, par. 217, 121.

³ Jung, *Mysterium Coniunctionis*, par. 736, 517.

⁴ See Jung's discussion of the *scintalla* in Jung, *Mysterium Coniunctionis*, par. 42–50, 48–56.

⁵ Jung, *Mysterium Coniunctionis*, par. 673, 472–473.

⁶ Jung, *Mysterium Coniunctionis*, par. 739, 519–520.

⁷ Jung, *Mysterium Coniunctionis*, par. 696, 489.

⁸ Jung, *Mysterium Coniunctionis*, par. 696, 489.

⁹ Jung, *Mysterium Coniunctionis*, par. 673, 472.

¹⁰ Jung, *Mysterium Coniunctionis*, par. 756, 531.

¹¹ Jung, *Mysterium Coniunctionis*, par. 742, 521.

¹² Jung, *Mysterium Coniunctionis*, par. 742, 521–522.

¹³ Dorn quoted in Jung, *Mysterium Coniunctionis*, par. 673, 472.

¹⁴ Jung, *Mysterium Coniunctionis*, par. 742, 521–522.

¹⁵ Jung, *Mysterium Coniunctionis*, par. 759, 533.

¹⁶ In a letter to R. F. C. Hull (December 27, 1958), Jung wrote: "Your suggestion to translate the subtitle of the *Mysterium Coniunctionis* as 'An Inquiry into the Fission and Fusion of Psychic Opposites in Alchemy' is indeed very clever. It is audacious and in a way profoundly right." A footnote to that letter explains, however, that "a fortnight later Jung changed his mind." He wrote to Hull: ". . . I had to think about your proposition. It is very witty indeed and I felt tempted to adopt it. But 'fission and fusion' are too specific to express the very general meaning of the

logical terms 'analysis and synthesis.'" See Jung, *Letters, Volume II: 1951–1961*, selected and edited by Gerald Adler and Aniela Jaffé (Princeton: Princeton University Press, 1976), 469–470.

[17] Jung, *Mysterium Coniunctionis*, par. 757, 532.

[18] See Jung, *Mysterium Coniunctionis*, par. 749, 526, for a discussion of the alchemical "recipe" for working with the unconscious using the method of active imagination.

[19] Jung, *Mysterium Coniunctionis*, par. 760, 534.

[20] Jung, *Aion*, par. 117, 64.

Afterword

As I look back on the years of my crisis of transformation now, more than two decades after it began, I am struck by the spontaneous emergence of imagery depicted in my dreams, synchronicities, and paintings that paralleled, often in striking detail, motifs in the alchemical treatises. Hundreds of years after the lives of the alchemists, the themes and experiences with which they had been concerned were reproduced within my own life in the twenty-first century. Studying my dreams and giving form to my experiences through painting helped me to discern the meaning underlying the disturbing and painful symptoms that afflicted me at that time, revealing the workings of an archetypal process of transformation and rebirth. The recognition of this meaning was perhaps the critical variable that enabled me to survive the experience and to understand it as a creative transition, of a spiritual nature, rather than a pathological decay into incapacitation and near-insanity. The dividing line between these two outcomes was often thin and permeable.

Towards the end of September 2004, as I was emerging from the crisis, in a journal entry I attempted to summarize what I had been through:

I have struggled long and hard with this mysterious process . . . that shattered my previous conceptions of life. I have experienced so many fluctuating states of consciousness, many of them harrowing. I have had to cultivate such intense self-discipline and will, to allow near-unbearable pain to burn out of my heart. I have grappled with the fear that my initial disintegration provoked and attempted to "swallow" the darkness, consciously seeking to move through into a new state of being. I have felt this as a real

191

experience, that of squeezing through, edging towards light from darkness, only then to be engulfed by more darkness. Each moment brought my old life and old self nearer to death. . . . I have had to develop new forms of self-control, training myself not to seek to avoid pain through action but instead to open my heart and absorb the full pain of all life situations, while overcoming the protestations of my inner being against this most taxing of impositions. The process has been relentless and times of peace fleeting. It has required near-constant attention, a superhuman effort from which I could not escape.

Although I continue to navigate the way of individuation and ongoing experiences of death-rebirth, and periodically find myself pulled back into the underworld, the sustained dark intensity of that initial period has mostly passed. My alchemical transformation did not deliver me to a state of blissful unity or contentment, as I had often hoped it might (perhaps this is a necessary delusion), but led me ever deeper into the conflict born of the tension of opposites, which has been the source of my knowledge of the psyche and my creative direction ever since. With the benefit of perspective, I came to see the crisis as a boon, affording me an understanding of the psyche one cannot get from books or even from psychotherapy. It also marked an initiation into a dramatically deeper mode of existence that called forth the development of a concentrated intensified consciousness and a refashioned ego, open to the biddings of the Self. For all the suffering it entailed, I came to recognize that the underworld struggle defined who I am and the work I have had to do in this life.

In a broader sense, what I became embroiled in, I believe, was a creative enactment, in microcosm, of the great spiritual drama playing itself out in our time. It is a drama marked by a critical evolutionary challenge that touches us all in one way or another: the reconciliation of the God of light with the dark spirit in nature, a reconciliation that is only possible through a transformation of the inner structure of the human personality. Alchemy, interpreted psychologically, can serve as a symbolic guide for those impelled, by choice or necessity, to face this challenge in their own lives.

Appendix:
An Extract from Mircea Eliade's
Interview with C. G. Jung for *Combat*

The following is an extract from Mircea Eliade's interview with C. G. Jung for *Combat* magazine, published in Paris on October 9th, 1952. A complete version of the interview is included in *C. G. Jung Speaking: Interviews and Encounters*, edited by William McGuire and R. F. C. Hull (London: Pan Books Ltd., 1980).

C. G. Jung: The great problem in psychology is the integration of opposites. One finds this everywhere and at every level. In *Psychology and Alchemy* (CW 12), I had occasion to interest myself in the integration of Satan. For, as long as Satan is not integrated, the world is not healed and man is not saved. But Satan represents evil, and how can evil be integrated? There is only one possibility: to assimilate it, that is to say, raise it to the level of consciousness. This is done by means of a very complicated symbolic process which is more or less identical with the psychological process of individuation. In alchemy this is called the conjunction of the two principles. As a matter of fact, alchemy actually takes up and carries on the work of Christianity. In the alchemical view, Christianity has saved man but not nature. The alchemist's dream was to save the world in its totality: the philosopher's stone was conceived as the *filius macrocosmi*, which saves the world, whereas Christ was the *filius microcosmi*, the savior of man alone. The ultimate aim of the alchemical opus is *apokatastasis*, cosmic salvation. . . .

Alchemy represents the projection of a drama both cosmic and spiritual in laboratory terms. The *opus magnum* had two aims: the rescue of the human soul and the salvation of the cosmos. What the alchemists called "matter" was in reality the [unconscious] self. The "soul of the world," the *anima mundi*, which was identified with the *spiritus mercurius*, was imprisoned in matter. It is for this reason the alchemists believed in the *truth* of "matter," because "matter" was actually their own psychic life. But it was a question of freeing this "matter," of saving it—in a word, of finding the philosopher's stone, the *corpus glorificationis*.

The work is difficult and strewn with obstacles; the alchemical opus is dangerous. Right at the beginning, you meet the "dragon," the chthonic spirit, the "devil" or, as the alchemists called it, the "blackness," the *nigredo*, and this encounter produces suffering. "Matter" suffers right up to the final disappearance of the blackness; in psychological terms, the soul finds itself in the throes of melancholy, locked in a struggle with the "shadow." The mystery of the *coniunctio*, the central mystery of alchemy, aims precisely at the synthesis of opposites, the assimilation of the blackness, the integration of the devil. For the "awakened" Christian this is a very serious psychic experience, for it is a confrontation with his own "shadow," with the blackness, the *nigredo*, which remains separate and can never be completely integrated into the human personality.

. . . .

On the psychological level, all these symbols and beliefs are interdependent: it is always a question of struggling with evil, with Satan, and conquering it, that is to say assimilating it, integrating it into consciousness. In the language of the alchemists, matter suffers until the *nigredo* disappears, when the "dawn" (*aurora*) will be announced by the "peacock's tail" (*cauda pavonis*), and a new day will break, the *leukosis* or *albedo*. But in this state of "whiteness" one does not *live* in the true sense of the word, it is a sort of abstract, ideal state. In order to make it come alive it must have "blood," it must have what the alchemists call the *rubedo*, the "redness" of life. Only the total experience of being can transform this ideal state of the *albedo* into a fully human mode of existence. Blood alone can reanimate a glorious state of consciousness in which the last trace of blackness is dissolved, in which the devil no longer has an autonomous existence but rejoins the profound unity of the psyche. Then the *opum magnum* is finished: the human soul is completed, integrated.

Bibliography

Assagioli, Roberto. *Transpersonal Development: The Dimension beyond Psychosynthesis*. London: The Aquarian Press, 1991.

Barnstone, Willis, and Marvin Meyer (editors). *The Gnostic Bible*. Revised and Expanded Edition. Boston, MA: Shambhala Publications, 2009.

Campbell, Joseph. *Creative Mythology: The Masks of God, Volume IV*. 1968. Repr., London: Arkana, 1995.

———. *The Hero with a Thousand Faces*. 1949. Repr., London: Fontana Press, 1993.

Campbell, Joseph, and Bill Moyers. *The Power of Myth*. 1988. Repr., New York: Anchor Books, 1991.

Edinger, Edward. *Anatomy of the Psyche: Alchemical Symbolism in Psychotherapy*. Peru, IL: Open Court, 1991.

Einstein, Albert. *The Born-Einstein Letters: Friendship, Politics and Physics in Uncertain Times*. Basingstoke, UK: Macmillan Press, 2005.

Eliade, Mircea. *The Forge and the Crucible: The Origins and Structures of Alchemy*. Second Edition. Chicago, IL: University of Chicago Press, 1979.

Freud, Sigmund. *New Introductory Lectures on Psycho-Analysis*. Standard edition. 1933. Translated by James Strachey. Repr., New York: W. W. Norton & Co., 1990.

Grof, Stanislav. *LSD Psychotherapy*. Alameda, CA: Hunter House, 1980.

———. *Psychology of the Future: Lessons from Modern Consciousness Research*. Albany, NY: State University of New York Press, 2000.

Jonas, Hans. *The Gnostic Religion: The Message of the Alien God and the Beginnings of Christianity*. Third edition. Boston, MA: Beacon Press, 2001.

Jung, Carl Gustav. *Aion: Researches into the Phenomenology of the Self.* Second edition. Volume 9, part II, of *The Collected Works of C. G. Jung*. Translated by R. F. C. Hull. Princeton: Princeton University Press, 1969.

———. *Alchemical Studies*. Volume 13 of *The Collected Works of C. G. Jung*. Translated by R. F. C. Hull. Princeton: Princeton University Press, 1967.

———. *Answer to Job. The Problem of Evil: Its Psychological and Religious Origins*. 1960. Translated by R. F. C. Hull. Repr., Cleveland, OH: Meridian Books, 1970.

———. *The Black Books*. Edited and Introduced by Sonu Shamdasani. Translated by Martin Liebscher, John Peck, and Sonu Shamdasani. New York: W. W. Norton & Co., 2020.

———. "Commentary on 'The Secret of the Golden Flower.'" In *Alchemical Studies*. Volume 13 of *The Collected Works of C. G. Jung*. Translated by R. F. C. Hull. Princeton: Princeton University Press, 1968.

———. "Concerning Rebirth." 1940/1950. In *The Archetypes and the Collective Unconscious*. Second edition. Volume 9, part I, of *The Collected Works of C. G. Jung*. Translated by R. F. C. Hull. Princeton: Princeton University Press, 1969.

———. "Eliade's Interview for 'Combat,'" with Mircea Eliade (from *Combat*, Paris, 1952). In *C. G. Jung Speaking: Interviews and Encounters*. Edited by William McGuire and R. F. C. Hull. London: Pan Books Ltd., 1980.

———. *Letters. Volume II: 1951–1961*. Selected and edited by Gerald Adler and Aniela Jaffé. Princeton: Princeton University Press, 1976.

———. *Memories, Dreams, Reflections*. 1963. Recorded and edited by Aniela Jaffé. Translated by Richard and Clara Wilson. Repr., London: Flamingo, 1983.

———. *Mysterium Coniunctionis: An Inquiry into the Separation and Synthesis of Psychic Opposites in Alchemy*. Second edition. Volume 14 of *The Collected Works of C. G. Jung*. Translated by R. F. C. Hull. Repr., Princeton: Princeton University Press, 1970.

———. "On Psychic Energy." 1948. In *On the Nature of the Psyche*. Translated by R. F. C. Hull. London and New York: Routledge, 2001.

———. "On the Psychology of the Unconscious." 1917/1926/1943. In *Two Essays on Analytical Psychology*. Second edition. Volume 7 of *The Collected Works of C. G. Jung*. Repr., London: Routledge, 1990.

———. "The Philosophical Tree." 1945/1954. In *Alchemical Studies*. Volume 13 of *The Collected Works of C. G. Jung*. Translated by R. F. C. Hull. Princeton: Princeton University Press, 1968.

———. *Psychology and Alchemy*. Second edition. Volume 12 of *The Collected Works of C. G. Jung*. Translated by R. F. C. Hull. Princeton: Princeton University Press, 1968.

———. *The Psychology of the Transference*. 1954/1966. Translated by R. F. C. Hull. Repr., Princeton: Princeton University Press, 1974.

———. *The Red Book: Liber Novus*. Edited and Introduced by Sonu Shamdasani. Translated by Mark Kyburz, John Peck, and Sonu Shamdasani. New York: W. W. Norton & Co., 2009.

———. "The Relations between the Ego and the Unconscious." 1928. In *Two Essays on Analytical Psychology*. Second edition. Volume 7 of *The Collected Works of C. G. Jung*. Repr., London: Routledge, 1990.

———. "Synchronicity: An Acausal Connecting Principle." 1952. In *The Structure and Dynamics of the Psyche*. Volume 8 of *The Collected Works of C. G. Jung*. Translated by R. F. C. Hull. London: Routledge & Kegan Paul, 1960/1969.

———. "Transformation Symbolism in the Mass." 1954. In *Psychology and Religion: West and East*. Volume 11 of *The Collected Works of C. G. Jung*. Translated by R. F. C. Hull. London: Routledge & Kegan Paul, 1958.

Le Grice, Keiron. *The Archetypal Cosmos: Rediscovering the Gods in Myth, Science and Astrology*. Edinburgh: Floris Books, 2011.

———. *The Rebirth of the Hero: Mythology as a Guide to Spiritual Transformation*. 2013. Repr., Ojai, CA: ITAS Publications, 2022.

Lyotard, Jacques. *The Postmodern Condition: A Report on Knowledge*. Translated by Geoff Bennington and Brian Massumi. Minneapolis, MN: Minnesota University Press, 1984.

Nietzsche, Friedrich. *Basic Writings of Nietzsche*. Translated by Walter Kaufmann. New York: The Modern Library, 2000.

———. *The Birth of Tragedy: Out of the Spirit of Music*. Translated by Shaun Whiteside. Edited by Michael Tanner. London: Penguin Books, 1993.

———. "Ecce Homo: How One Becomes What One Is." In *Basic Writings of Nietzsche*. Translated and edited by Walter Kaufmann. New York: The Modern Library, 2000.

———. *The Gay Science: With a Prelude in Rhymes and an Appendix of Songs*. Translated by Walter Kaufmann. New York: Vintage Books, 1974.

———. *Thus Spoke Zarathustra*. Translated by Richard J. Hollingdale. New York: Penguin, 1969.

Pagels, Elaine. *The Gnostic Gospels*. New York: Vintage Books, 1979.

Roob, Alexander. *Alchemy & Mysticism*. Cologne, Germany: Taschen, 2015.

Ross, Hugh McGregor, trans. *The Gospel of Thomas*. London: Watkins Publishing, 2002.

www.ingramcontent.com/pod-product-compliance
Lightning Source LLC
Chambersburg PA
CBHW050805270326
41926CB00025B/4544